CONFESSIONS
of a GYPSY YOGINI

RANGJUNG YESHE BOOKS □ WWW.RANGJUNG.COM

PADMASAMBHAVA □ *Treasures from Juniper Ridge* □ *Advice from the Lotus-Born* □ *Dakini Teachings*

PADMASAMBHAVA AND JAMGÖN KONGTRÜL □ *The Light of Wisdom, 2 vols.*

YESHE TSOGYAL □ *The Lotus-Born*

DAKPO TASHI NAMGYAL □ *Clarifying the Natural State*

TSELE NATSOK RANGDRÖL □ *Mirror of Mindfulness* □ *Empowerment* □ *Heart Lamp*

CHOKGYUR LINGPA □ *Ocean of Amrita* □ *The Great Gate* □ *Skillful Grace*

JAMGÖN MIPHAM RINPOCHE □ *Gateway to Knowledge, 3 vols.*

TULKU URGYEN RINPOCHE □ *Blazing Splendor* □ *Rainbow Painting* □ *As It Is, 2 vols.* □ *Vajra Speech* □ *Repeating the Words of the Buddha*

KHENCHEN THRANGU RINPOCHE □ *Crystal Clear* □ *Songs of Naropa* □ *King of Samadhi* □ *Buddha Nature*

CHÖKYI NYIMA RINPOCHE □ *Present Fresh Wakefulness* □ *Indisputable Truth* □ *Union of Mahamudra & Dzogchen* □ *Bardo Guidebook* □ *Song of Karmapa*

TSIKEY CHOKLING RINPOCHE □ *Lotus Ocean*

TULKU THONDUP □ *Enlightened Living*

ORGYEN TOBGYAL RINPOCHE □ *Life & Teachings of Chokgyur Lingpa*

DZIGAR KONGTRUL □ *Uncommon Happiness*

TSOKNYI RINPOCHE □ *Fearless Simplicity* □ *Carefree Dignity*

DZOGCHEN TRILOGY COMPILED BY MARCIA BINDER SCHMIDT □ *Dzogchen Primer* □ *Dzogchen Essentials* □ *Quintessential Dzogchen*

ERIK PEMA KUNSANG □ *Wellsprings of the Great Perfection* □ *A Tibetan Buddhist Companion* □ *The Rangjung Yeshe Tibetan-English Dictionary of Buddhist Culture*

CONFESSIONS
of a GYPSY YOGINI

Experience through Mistakes

MARCIA DECHEN WANGMO

Foreword by
TULKU THONDUP

Edited with
MEGHAN HOWARD

Rangjung Yeshe Publications
Boudhanath, Hong Kong & Esby
2010

Rangjung Yeshe Publications
Flat 5a, Greenview Garden
125 Robinson Road, Hong Kong

Address letters to:
Rangjung Yeshe Publications
P.O. Box 1200
Kathmandu, Nepal

Internet homepage: *www.rangjung.com*

FIRST EDITION 2010
Printed in the United States of America

1 3 5 7 9 8 6 4 2

PUBLICATION DATA:

ISBN 978-9-62-734164-2

COVER ART: DESIGN: Maryan Lipaj
FRONT AND BACK COVER ART: Chitfu Yu

Contents

Foreword

THE FOLLOWERS OF MAHAYANA BUDDHISM view the two truths as the foundation, dedicate their lives to training in the two accumulations as the path, and attain the twofold buddha body as the goal to fulfill the needs of themselves and others. This is the basic spectrum of most of the trainings enshrined in this book.

Foundation: Followers view all that exists—mind and matter—all that appears to the mind of ordinary beings arises and functions through the law of interdependent causation, and that is the relative truth. The true nature of all that is realized by enlightened wisdom is emptiness (or openness), free from duality and true existence, and that is the absolute truth. How they appear and what they are is the unity of all things as their true qualities and true nature.

Path: Followers train in meritorious deeds, the first five perfections, by studying, analyzing, and meditating on them to complete the accumulation of merit. They train in the emptiness (or openness) that is the nature of everything, the sixth perfection, to complete the accumulation of wisdom. Every serious Buddhist student must advance through the path of twofold accumulation.

Some followers advance along the path swiftly, others slowly, while yet others fall off or can't get on. All depends on their dedication, the faculties that they enjoy, and the degree to which their minds are open. Through esoteric paths such as Dzogpa Chenpo and Mahamudra, meditators can awaken their own innate nature, the awareness-wisdom, instantly. However, to reach such a possibility, a stream of efforts is required for a long time. In Buddhism, there are infinite approaches to suit the infinite mental makeup of limitless beings. These approaches all share the common aim of awakening one's own enlightened nature—the total awareness. The clearer and fuller followers' awakenings, the greater degree of peace, joy, and omniscience they will enjoy. That, in turn, enables them to share what they are enjoying with others with greater power.

Goal: By awakening the awareness-wisdom fully, followers attain the spontaneously present ultimate body of Buddhahood—the union of the ultimate sphere and primordial wisdom, pure from its origin and free from any adventitious obscuration. By perfecting the merits fully, they embody two form bodies of Buddhahood. Through the ever-present fivefold certainties of the Enjoyment body they serve the enlightened ones of the tenth stage. Through the infinite display of Manifested body, they serve infinite unenlightened beings as long as any remain to be served.

Confessions of a Gypsy Yogini is a vivifying account of the ambrosia-like Buddhist path with the brilliant imagery and clear voices of many renowned masters recorded by the author, who herself lived for seventeen years at the feet of one of the greatest Tibetan masters of meditation at the epicenter of unfolding events of Dharma that crossed many oceans. May this volume reach many to ignite the light of love and wisdom—the true meaning of Dharma—in their hearts.

Tulku Thondup

Marcia in Nangchen, Tibet 2003

Marcia Dechen Wangmo

Introduction

THIS BOOK IS NOT A SUCCESS STORY; it is a snapshot of a work in progress, offered with enthusiasm and associated insight. In a traditional presentation, I would give my Dharma history, my teachers, the lineages and teachings I have received, and the practices I have done, and note my years in retreat to instill confidence in what you are about to read. I would be self-effacing, expressing my arrogance even to undertake such an endeavor, especially since I have not imbibed any of the qualities of all those teachers, lineages, teachings, and retreats. So, I will begin by confessing it is indeed true I have had manifold opportunities and the good fortune to progress, laziness and all the other accompanying negative thought states have waylaid me. I have *almost* given up on myself, but maybe all the instructions I have received from great teachers will help someone else. Of course, the teachings help me when I practice them; I am not hindered by any aspect of the teachings themselves, but by my lack of applying them. Granted there is potential for triumph, but it has not happened yet. As an aspiring yogini[1], I feel that my frank observations might serve some purpose. Having been requested many times by friends to share my experiences, I offer this book with as much pure motivation as someone like me can muster, as a sketch of a landscape wondrously traveled.

I can confirm the path because, even with all my setbacks and failures, what I have been introduced to and what I wish to unfurl is the strength of our spirit, the confidence in our capability as human beings. We ordinary people can rise above our constraints and upbringings to change in positive ways. We can connect with our most pure basic nature and triumph over any challenge. You see, no matter who we are, we are already complete and perfect, but have not yet linked with this innate potential in our beings. This is what we need to hook up with in order to heal our fractured selves that have fallen into despondency and panic. My relentless determination is guided by experience, both personal and, most strongly, by association. I have been around people who took hold of their inner potential and were shining lights in an age of darkness.

You may wonder, how did a regular American girl step onto this path and into this lifestyle? There were no signs or guiding factors in my background to indicate a proclivity to spiritual life. In fact, my early years were so uneventful and mundane that I was sure I had landed in the wrong place or that there had been a mix-up at the hospital where I was born. Somehow I felt that my circumstances were flawed, but because I lacked any points of reference, I could not ascertain what might be missing.

One of my very earliest recollections is at four years old sitting in our family living room in full lotus, a yogic cross-legged posture, and understanding that nobody noticed or had any interest in what I was doing. Although I thought it was a bit odd, I was just a kid and did not hold on to perceptions or memories for very long. Later, as I grew up I had various inexplicable experiences that were not identifiable in my normal context. During my teenage years, I was unimpressed by mundane life and the commonly accepted reality of everyday living. These were the pre-hippie years, so it is difficult to give an accurate description of my early indoctrination and my reaction to it.

At seventeen, I was working as a volunteer in a local hospital when I had an epiphany while swirling down a circular staircase. The idea arose that I would get enlightened to benefit beings. Nothing preceded it, yet it was the birth of the noble

Buddhist attitude within me. This remarkable thought arose instinctively and I knew, spontaneously and unprompted by outside influences, that I was a Buddhist practitioner. Amusingly, one day many years later I went back to the hospital to revisit the scene of my transformation. As I strolled through the lobby, I could not locate the staircase and questioned the receptionist if they had remodeled and she said yes. I asked why they had done away with the staircase; her response was that "there never was a staircase here." Staircase or not, my epiphany was an extremely clear occurrence that has stayed with me my whole life because, without any external pressure or prodding, I had awakened to the mind of enlightenment. There had come a moment of opening and realization in my being that later teachings and trainings I came into contact with identified as an integral part of the Buddhist path. In retrospect, the thoughts of not belonging, of not being in the right place, of being different from other people, and various peculiar childhood occurrences were indications that I met had the Dharma in a past life. There was no influence from my family or my environment to account for these feelings. I can only surmise that this was the ripening of my own experience at the appropriate time, coming from previous lives. It doesn't mean that I am anyone special—quite the opposite—but the teachings say that none of us would even be able to meet the Dharma in this life if we had not formerly done so.

Somehow this good fortune, which survived various personas in my current life (quasi student radical, hippie, horse trainer, and environmentalist, all of which I will reference at different times)[2], surfaced to guide me to seek out and eventually meet the Buddhist teachings and my teacher, Tulku Urgyen Rinpoche, one of the most accomplished Dzogchen yogis of recent times. I cannot speak of his realization, but I can speak about his immense compassion, enthusiasm, and humility. Coming into his presence, one entered an effluence of empathy and love. As his students can concur, by his behavior and especially his teachings, he made recognition[3] of mind nature seem so easy and natural. His assurance of our ability was so strong; it was contagious. Like the warmth of sunlight, he emanated love that opened us up. This strength and affection was limitless. We all wanted to be like him and embody the qualities he possessed with such extreme humbleness. He perfected high view, low profile. His view and conduct were impeccable.

What really distinguished Tulku Urgyen Rinpoche and illustrated his sincere humility and kindness was how he greeted everyone he met. Most high lamas will acknowledge you by giving a blessing with their hand, a ritual object, a book, a statue, or a long-life arrow. Tulku Urgyen Rinpoche touched heads with each person who came into his presence. Such a gesture from a realized being was a remarkable confirmation of being equal and accepted. He did not entertain any concepts of high or low, clean or unclean. Each person who journeyed to meet him was worthy in his eyes to be welcomed with respect and impartiality. As he bowed in response to each of us, he was joyously expressing his love for all people.

Tulku Urgyen Rinpoche was among the first Tibetan masters to teach the most essential instructions of Dzogchen outside Tibet. He conveyed the Dzogchen instructions with brilliance, and was famed for profound meditative realization and the concise, lucid, and humorous style with which he imparted these teachings. His method was "instruction through one's own experience." Using few words, he pointed out the nature of mind[4], revealing a natural simplicity of wakefulness that enabled the student to touch the heart of enlightenment. He changed the lives of many of the Buddhist practitioners who found their way to Nagi Nunnery, his hermitage above the Kathmandu Valley.

According to Rinpoche's teachings, the core of the Buddhist path is to contact our own true essence. The path unfolds in a practical, applicable way that fosters happiness and well-being, avoiding negativity and misery. An advanced science of body and mind, it offers methods of scrutinizing behavior, actions, and their results. We can learn to explore how our minds work without becoming too emotionally involved in what unfolds. We can discover how to judge intelligently what is and what is not beneficial, and find out how to trust the openness and our own potential. Then we can actually meet our inherent nature face to face and engage in training to sustain it. This is what we have been avoiding. We have fostered an inability to recognize that which is within us. There is nothing superior to this essential nature, and it is not found anywhere else than inside.

If this is the case, what happened? How was that which could not be lost, misplaced? In fact, it is never lost; it is merely hidden and will remain so until the layers of unknowing that cover the basic state are stripped away. There is a fundamental need to come into direct and unwavering contact with our buddha nature and that which prevents us is dualistic, grasping mind and its conditioned mental processes. There is an underlying uneasiness that subtly permeates our experience. An unconscious watcher writes the script, unaware of true inner brilliance. To shield and protect this unawareness, it tries various scenarios to create a seemingly comfortable perspective, offering the distractions of drugs, alcohol, meditation, New-Age spirituality, entertainment, politics, and sports.

Anything that takes us away from the openness of the present moment is a viable option. We can spend our whole lifetime straying further and further from it. We project our natural energy outwardly, looking after others, watching the kids grow, minding the garden, fixing the house, and working. There is nothing wrong with any of this; but it is simply not enough for the spiritually inclined person. To apprehend this can cause us to seek answers in different places. Here is the irony: all we need to know is how to meet our own inner nature. We have to start outside ourselves to do so.

Confession, in the context of this book, is not an exposure of juicy details but an admission of my faults and inability to act with correct conduct according to the teachings. By exposing my shortcomings, I hope they may become a conduit for my readers to explore and engage correctly. The book's subtitle, *experience through mistakes,* means learning the hard way—mostly by error, even when intellectually knowing better—and not trying to deny this. In difficult situations, often I have a good understanding of the Dharma, but fail to live it or apply it. Only when these difficulties smash me over the head do I pay attention and wake up. I cannot claim to possess the special qualities needed to intercept mindfulness moment-to-moment.

Perhaps the example of the places where I have strayed from the path will serve as a warning for others. Hence, I present this work as a memoir-guidebook to help others as well as myself. It is a paper mirror, reflecting advice and methods, and it is a forum for questioning the image in that mirror. Each topic in this book is discussed according to a framework of processes revealed by the Buddha. I trust that it will draw you closer to seeing things as they truly are, helping you to ascertain and validate your inherent beauty, find the positive, and overcome the negative. First, we need to study our confusion and then investigate the tools to clear some of it away. We begin the road to healing by learning how to meditate. As we journey along, there will be many techniques offered. We will see how to dissociate with the careless, selfish people we have become. Hopefully we will realize how our enemies—fluctuating thoughts and perceptions—have consumed and tricked us, and we will learn to examine, disavow, and triumph over them.

By training in simple formulas, we can glimpse a vast openness free of unhappiness, and learn to deal with our experiences. Ultimately, we can realize how to benefit others. This does seem like a lot to offer in such a small book without a warranty. Nevertheless, it can happen, or at least begin to happen. How much we apply the trainings and how seriously we undergo the challenges is up to us.

Finally, I must add that what distinguishes my experience from that of others who share my ordinary background and upbringing is that, after a number of years spent dabbling with meditation practice and various lifestyles, I made a conscious choice to dedicate my life to the spiritual path and to help beings through that effort. I wish I could say that I definitively decided to abandon worldly aims and samsaric pursuits, but things were not that clear-cut. I mixed both existences. Now, thirty years later, as I still play with conditioned realities and am not fully convinced of their futility, I have at least recognized that there is nothing more profound, precious, and meaningful than the Dharma. My trust in the teachers, the teachings, and their intrinsic value continuously increases and is resolute. Even though I cannot offer any wondrous experiences of realization, I can at least offer this trust with the unqualified joy of having found a path and met true guides along it. The Dharma is most certainly an extraordinary gift that asks for nothing in return except to open to it with our hearts and minds.

Paradise Lost

*I confess to not cutting confused experience at
the root.*

WHEN I FIRST CAME IN CONTACT with the Buddhadharma
and heard that the primary reason to enter its path is because of
suffering, I rejected that explanation. Suffering is not the first
word that came to my mind to describe my life—the Buddha
must have been referring to someone else. I was looking to escape
the mundane, ordinarily accepted reality that, though uninterest-
ing, was not unbearable. Over the years, however, rejecting the
idea of suffering has been a pretty hard line to toe, since the truth
of suffering is the first of the Four Noble Truths taught by the
Buddha.[5] Although I cannot deny that pain and suffering are experienced by myself and other beings, I do not feel that it is the
primary motivating factor that brought me to the Dharma. Am I
deluded to think that I came to the Dharma through the strength
of my personal conviction to strive for realization in an altruistic
way? Am I denying weakness, and is pain weakness? If anything,
what do I really need to renounce?

Lately, I have concluded that the mistake lies with trans-
lating the word *duhkha* as "suffering." It is more than the fear of
suffering that brings most of us to the Buddhist path. Perhaps
more subtle thought states like weariness, disillusionment and
uneasiness could better represent the motivating factor. It is an
active choice that transcends gross psychological turmoil and personal pain. We somehow glimpse, by the virtue of buddha nature, a deep-seated understanding that acknowledges the futility

9

of ordinary existence. Our disappointment lets us understand the pointlessness of worldly pursuits. Duhkha connotes the underlying mental anxieties fueled by attempts to protect our unawareness. We bear the worry of needing to be in charge, though we have lost control.

The continual churning of thoughts is exhausting. We are weary of conditioned existence. The faint undercurrent of all our experiences, both good and bad, is transitory in nature. We move apprehensively in a maze of subjective, projected reality, always trying to make things be all right. Because we are so often outwardly driven, we don't even recognize our basic hesitation. Instead, we take hold of anything to shield us from our inner dialogue.

According to Western psychology, maladapted states of mind are unwholesome patterns that develop from a variety of causes, the most prevalent of which are early close relationships and unwholesome integration with the larger world. Unhealthy states of mind pertain to some trauma or mistreatment, emotional or physical. The causes are very much associated with this life only.

Buddhist psychology looks at a much subtler cause: the basic inability to experience reality as it is. It is this primary unknowing that is the root of all our problems. It begins with ignorance and continues to solidify the world based on delusion. In particular, our obscured perception develops into a strong misconception that grasps a solid self. There are no easy ways to explain this primary misapprehension. As Tulku Urgyen Rinpoche explains,

> Wisdom is extremely subtle, and we need to understand it in a very subtle way. It doesn't help to have a gross understanding. But when we discuss, we need to use words. Without words we can't explain anything. That is why we use the terms *the way it is* and *the way it appears*. These two are a unity, and we, as sentient beings, have

separated them and therefore do not attain the unified level of ultimate realization. The reason why they aren't unified is because we separate the two through dualistic fixation on subject and object. We regard object as being out there and the consciousness as being in here. And by fixating on the consciousness as being within, we make the program for the outer perceived object and the inner perceiving mind. So by having fixated on the inner consciousness, it turns into the five poisons and the outer objects, manifest as being form, smell, sight, taste, sound, and texture, the five elements. In this way we are unsuccessful.[6]

It is the basic state, the ground[7], the original purity, which ordinary beings have not acknowledged. The cause of delusion is ignorance, which comes from what Thinley Norbu Rinpoche calls "the circumstance of lack of recognition of awareness."[8] He continues, "According to the Great Perfection, it can be called not recognizing the self-manifesting appearance of the natural emanation of self-occurring awareness. Since it is not recognized, it is held as other and delusion starts."[9]

Trungpa Rinpoche defines this ignorance as

the fundamental sense of ignoring oneself . . . Once there is bewilderment, a sort of double take begins to happen of wanting to find out where you were, what you are, where you are at. But the nature of bewilderment is that you do not want to go back and find out your original, you do not want to undo everything and go back. Since there is bewilderment there is something to latch onto, you want to ignore the case history

that led to that altogether. You want to make the
best of the present moment and cling to it.[10]

Unlike us, the Buddha met this delusion head on and
traced it back to its origin. When we accept that we are anxious
and unfulfilled, we enter upon a spiritual path to eradicate the
trepidation and fill in the gap. As Trungpa Rinpoche writes,
"From the Buddhist point of view, this search is evidence of basic
sanity operating within neurosis: almost an instinct to find an answer to our confusion."[11]

Before proceeding, we need to unravel the net of misunderstanding and "find the original." We need to go back to the
beginning of the story of mind, to find where we went wrong and
how it happened. Habituated to dualism, we perpetuate a mistaken reality of "me" and "other" to our detriment over countless
lifetimes. Investigating the basis of this misguided phenomenon
and acknowledging this faulty experience opens the door to its
transformation.

Before I relate my understanding of Buddhist psychological and philosophical teaching, it would be good to establish
the need for seeing how any of this is relevant to our present way
of experiencing and behaving. We are caught up in the web of
mistaken perception, we connect to reality like the characters in
Hans Christian Andersen's "The Emperor's New Clothes." We
buy into the generally accepted version of truth and become accustomed to it. First, we need to question our grasping to this
mistaken certainty. Buddhism is a study of the science of self.
Each vehicle offers different tools and methods to pull away the
illusion and connect to the way things actually are. The closer
we get to enlightened mind, the subtler the teachings become. It
helps to begin by investigating and analyzing the aggregates.[12]

On the grossest level, we have developed a strong habit
of ego[13] based on the previously mentioned lack of primordial

recognition. From the lack of knowing, fear arises. We then constrict the openness of the basic state, our enlightened essence, and strangle it like space held in our hands. Having solidified space, we bump into it and are intimidated. The vastness becomes frozen. We encase our basic nature in self and not-self (other). This corresponds to the first of the five aggregates, that of form.[14]

The self is characterized by its impressions, needing to structure personal terrain to fit its needs. This occurs before there is a conscious act of doing anything, as unawareness influences and molds our mode of reacting. This is not a verbal or cognitive action, but only a movement within the proud maze of tunnel vision. Although we encapsulate space on a primary level, the world outside of this elemental falsification is not necessarily a very friendly place. We judge all situations in terms of benefit or harm, "me" being of primary importance. This corresponds to the second of the five aggregates, that of sensations.[15]

Now that we have fortified the self, we can confidently place ourselves in the center of the mandala of experience and react to what pleases or threatens us. We grasp at distinguishing things. We further strengthen our position by firing up the energy of attraction. We have covered the space with earth and now need to heat this up to survive in our attachment. We manipulate every situation, utilizing the possibilities for our own means. This corresponds to the third of the five aggregates, that of perception.[16]

Even though others do not figure prominently in our personal landscape, they are still present. From our narrow relative viewpoint, we begin to struggle with our perceived challengers, needing to create a new order. In comparison to ourselves, we see them in a much more swift and turbulent way, and we plot how to best these opponents. Having lost the warmth of appreciation, a cool wind of competitiveness blows in the background. This corresponds to the fourth of the five aggregates, that of formations.[17]

We have now arrived at a fully identified self that needs to be protected by any means. We objectify all that happens. A strong division between the "I" and "other phenomena" necessitates keeping boundaries that must be fiercely guarded. It is like the torrent of a raging river, water flooding everywhere without mercy. An intellect that can fortify and protect itself by active engagement is the last development of ego. This corresponds to the fifth of the five aggregates, that of consciousness.[18]

These five aspects comprise the physical and mental constituents of any sentient being, and are maintained by the transitory shape of thoughts. The chapter on meditation will explain this in more detail. For now, it is sufficient to say that the aggregates are complex and made up of many parts. Though we might not recognize them individually, they program us to experience in erroneous ways. Predominance of any one of these five tendencies is how beings undergo each of the six realms of existence. Out of control, these negative patterns lead to different rebirths: ignorance as an animal, greed as a hungry ghost, pride as a god, jealousy as an *asura,* attachment as a human, and anger as a hell being.

Even in the course of a day, we live out each of these thought patterns or "realms," which persist in our daily experience, whether we accept their existence or not. We lack awareness in many situations, and our dullness obscures our abilities, like animals muzzled or leashed. We are selfish and proud, holding our needs over those of others, each time more concerned with ourselves. How often do we find ourselves unable to rejoice in the achievements of others, envying their good fortune and denigrating their achievements? Our compulsion to manipulate and dominate situations leads to endless disappointments, as we are under the power of causes and conditions and stifled by karma. Either the aggression of our out-of-control emotional viewpoint inflames our antagonism, or steel-cold indifference freezes our landscape.

The good news is that each of these confused states has a

wisdom side. It is too early to talk about that right now, because we must understand confused experience before we can eliminate it. Anyway, the beauty of the Dharma is that in every situation there is light at the end of the tunnel and a map that leads us there.

Let's backtrack a bit and reiterate some of what has been said. Whether we look at it from the perspective of time without beginning or in this present moment, we have the possibility to awaken to our true nature. We possess an enlightened essence, but having temporarily lost that connection we are deluded. Continuously missing the opportunity to awaken, we fall under the power of our ordinary experience, governed by habits so strenuous to maintain such as clinging to a self. Even from a mundane perspective, if we just stop holding on to our narrow viewpoint, and let it drop, we can redefine our perspective, seeing an enemy as a teacher for example. Then there is great freedom and possibility. The loosening of our grasping untangles a knot in our heart; we do not need to stay bound and strangled by it. Likewise, from our confused state, we can be reprogrammed because we are primordially enlightened and we have the potential to return to that state as re-enlightened.

Best to leave this for now and conclude by using Tulku Urgyen Rinpoche's words:

> We have failed to recognize the buddha nature [defined previously as self-occurring awareness] that is present in everyone. This ignorance is the main cause for straying into confusion. Sentient beings have strayed into confusion, like a precious jewel that has fallen into the mud and is temporarily unrecognizable.
>
> All the attempts to clean the jewel in order to re- move the dirt obscuring it are the example for

spiritual practices that enable one to gain realization. The dirt has to be removed to re-establish
the purity of the jewel. We are like jewels scattered in different places: equal quality, but separate pieces. Some jewels were lucky. Some fell in
the mud.[19]

Red or Blue Pill

I confess to attaching substance to the insubstantial
cycle of existence.

OUR BUDDHA NATURE is our innate legacy, our vital core and fundamental condition, which, when fully realized and stabilized, is no different from the enlightened mind of all the buddhas. We simply need to open to recognizing and reconnecting with our original, essential state. So, where do we ordinary people begin, if we assume that we are deceived and deluded, wandering around in an imperfect situation? Even if we partially accept that assumption, how can we be sure not to merely continue our illusory facade that takes the fictitious for the genuine?

To transcend confusion, we need to generate a profound conviction that we can truly do so. To bring about these circumstances, we need to make sincere, deeply felt aspirations to encounter a true teacher and genuine teachings that can rouse us out of our stupor and serve as a conduit to contact our basic wisdom. Currently, it is our lack of merit or good fortune that prevents us from taking hold of this inborn inheritance.

Let us begin by acknowledging that we can generate this merit by intending, purely and strongly, to engage in spirituality. Following are some important guidelines for making these wishes and forming the resolve to be able to enter the spiritual path:

1. Comprehend that we are able to reach Buddhahood because we possess the enlightened essence that is perfect and complete within us.

2. Dismantle doubts and concepts that prevent this acceptance by intellectually disassembling our most basic misconceptions (belief in a truly existing self and the substantiality of phenomena).
3. Form the determination to tread the path of awakening, and generate the heartfelt objective to stick to it.
4. Engender compassion for all other confused beings harboring this delusion and, bringing them into your experiential field, consider them with empathy and arouse a powerful determination to benefit them.
5. Seek a qualified teacher to accept and direct you.

We possess within us the enlightened essence that is perfect and complete.

If we didn't have the wish-fulfilling jewel of buddha nature, no amount of cleansing would make a difference. The diverse Buddhist practices are trainings meant to bring us back to our basic state, our inherent, enlightened jewel-essence. As we are ultimately perfect, we need to develop confidence that our efforts can lead to that fruition. We can accomplish amazing goals for infinite benefit, because our essential nature is emptiness with a core of awareness and the expression of that is insight, love, and compassion. We merely haven't come to terms with this aspect of ourselves. As Dilgo Khyentse Rinpoche comments:

> We all have this buddha nature, it is fundamental to us. If the mind were not primordially pure, it would be quite impossible to make it pure, just as it is impossible to extract gold from ordinary rock, however much one breaks it up and tries to melt and refine it. But just as refining gold ore by

washing, melting, and beating it will eventually produce gold, striving on the path will unveil the nature of enlightenment, which has been with us from the very beginning. This is precisely why we can attain enlightenment. If that perfectly pure absolute nature were not already present within us, there would be no way to create it by exerting ourselves on the path.

In the same way, the view, meditation, and action related to the absolute nature are present within one's being. By unveiling this absolute nature through practice, one can actualize Buddhahood. Now we need to recognize the buddha nature through practice, like making fire by striking steel and flint in the presence of tinder. We can attain Buddhahood because its nature is intrinsic to us. It is important to understand this and put it into practice.[20]

Disassemble misconceptions about the truly existing self and the substantiality of phenomena.

We misapprehend reality, closely identifying with our concepts of self: my body, my mind, my thoughts, my feelings, and my perceptions. This unwise grasping is one of our foremost predicaments and needs to be released. We should start by entertaining a healthy skepticism about all you pigeonhole as being exactly as you think it is. Dream is the perfect analogy to elucidate this. Whatever takes place at night while sleeping seems very real, yet when we wake, it all vanishes. We cannot say that those experiences did not happen, because we underwent them, but we cannot say that they exist in a concrete way, because they disappear when we wake.

One solidly ingrained, mistaken certainty is in an intrinsically existing self. We put so much effort into protecting our idea of personal identity, we want to trust that all we hold dear and strive for has an actual, substantial existence. We reify all our experiences, when in fact they are illusory. The five primary negative emotions (anger, pride, attachment, jealousy, and stupidity) have as their basis clinging to "me" as most important.

We need to unravel the ego. One way to do this is by working on the perception of egolessness in accordance with the first set of Buddha's teachings on developing insight into lack of self. In the second set of teachings, the Buddha went even further than explaining the nonexistence of the self; he revealed the nonexistence of all phenomena. All things are inherently empty. Thrangu Rinpoche elucidates the Buddha's skillful means to combat the misconception of nothingness: "Not only is the identity of all things empty; it is emptiness itself. This emptiness by nature has the capacity to know, to experience, to cognize. That is the wakeful wisdom quality that is indivisible from emptiness itself and is the intent of the final turning of the Wheel of Dharma."[21] Whether buddhas appear on this earth or not, the essence of phenomena never changes. The Buddha taught the way things truly are, drawing our attention to these undeniable truths. It is precisely because of emptiness that all phenomena can unfold. The empty accommodates everything and provides the possibility for the unfolding.

> *The various forms of suffering are like the death of one's*
> *   child in a dream:*
> *By clinging to deluded perceptions as real we exhaust ourselves.*
> *Therefore, when encountering unfavorable circumstances,*
> *To view them as illusions is the practice of a bodhisattva.*[22]

Form the determination to tread upon the path of awakening.

Anyway, we are stuck in the mud. We approach the decisive juncture where we decide whether to climb out or to remain stuck. In the movie the *Matrix,* the skilled hero Morpheus offers Neo, the future hero, an option between two pills, one red and one blue. Taking the blue pill would eradicate his memory of all that has been revealed to him about the fallacious reality he inhabits. He would simply fade away into gleeful oblivion and nonaction. Taking the red pill would awaken him to the unadulterated, genuine way things are. He would be motivated to engage in the struggle to transform the world for those asleep in the deception.

We are at an analogous crossroad: Take the red pill, determine to apply Dharma methods, and begin a fresh, traditional, radical course. Taking the red pill acknowledges our bewilderment and introduces the possibility of a vast attitude directed toward the ultimate fruition, complete enlightenment. Free from all deluded and painful states, we are infused with wisdom and the capacity to benefit countless beings. No matter what has happened to us in the past, it is gone, finished. We no longer need to keep the tortured memories of abuse, stupidity, or unhappiness by replaying and churning over them continuously. Understand and identify the distress and stop nurturing it; progress onwards. The choice is ours at any moment to take hold of our mind and direct it in any way we decide. Dzongsar Khyentse Rinpoche calls this starting point "renunciation mind":

> That I easily become annoyed and agitated shows that I do not have renunciation mind. Renunciation mind is very simple in a way. We have renunciation mind when we realize that all this is not a big deal. Somebody steps on your toe,

what's the big deal? The more we get used to this notion, the more we have renunciation mind. At least I try to see why I make all this into such a big deal. I am merely giving you a model of how to invoke renunciation mind.

It is a bit like this example. We have been walking in this desert for so long, and anything that flows, anything that is watery, is so important for us. Even if we see a mirage our only wish is to get near the water without ever realizing that it is a mirage. If you don't know that it is a mirage and you go there, all you end up with is a big disappointment. So, knowing that it is only a mirage is renunciation mind. . . .

Renunciation somehow has this connotation of giving something up. But it is like the example of the mirage. You can't give up the water because there is none; it is only a mirage. Moreover, you don't have to give up a mirage because what is the point of giving up a mirage; one need simply know that it is a mirage. Such understanding is a big renunciation. The moment you know that it is a mirage, most likely you will not even go there because you know it is fake; or even if you do go, there is no disappointment because you already know what is there. At the very least you will only have a little disappointment. That is why Jamgon Kongtrul said renunciation mind is like a foundation. . . .

Renunciation mind has nothing to do with sacrificing. As I just mentioned, when we talk about renunciation, somehow we get all scared because we think that we have to give up some goodies, something valuable, some important things. But there is nothing that is important; there is nothing that solidly exists. All that you are giving up is actually a vague identity. You realize that this is not true, not the ultimate, and this is how and why to develop renunciation.[23]

It may seem outlandish, but we behave like children chasing after illusory rainbows. We hold that our conditioned existence is able to grant us contentment, and we tirelessly pursue that phantom joy. In reality, it is a deception as constant and enduring as a sand castle built on the ocean's shore. We do not obtain anything but dissatisfaction and frustration, yet we cannot surrender our deep-seated certainty that samsara has value. Renunciation seems like such a sacrifice, but as Dzongsar Khyentse Rinpoche remarks, we are not abandoning anything except the fantasy. There is not any authenticity in worldly phenomena, no matter how hard we endeavor to substantiate them. To enter the spiritual path is not to be deprived of all that is meaningful and worthwhile; it is the opposite. We embrace the meaningful and worthwhile, and recognize the futility of everything else.

Engender compassion.

Allegorically, accepting these ideas or even being influenced somewhat by their validity, is to swallow the red pill; you chart a fresh but well-proven course. Your perspective is realigned, and innovative vistas can open. With this new revelation, you have the knowledge to scrutinize your immediate environment, and, unfortunately, it is distressing. Not only have you not triumphed miraculously and instantaneously over unhappiness, frustration, and lack of fulfillment, but you discern that almost everyone else you know is subtly dissatisfied and uneasy with their reality as well. You have developed a sharp sensitivity that cannot avoid confronting this. You are compelled to do something radical to benefit all these other hapless beings.

There are many eminent approaches to overcoming bewilderment. One of the most effective is to generate sincere compassion for all unfortunate, deluded beings. Step out of the mold of egotism and expand your heart. Stop focusing on "me," and promote transformation, determine to make a departure from the norm. I will go into detail about some of these practices a few chapters from now. Here I would like to relate the experience of one of my teachers, Adeu Rinpoche, to illustrate the futility of focusing only on oneself.

Rinpoche spent many years in a Chinese prison camp in Xining, one of the harshest in all Tibet. It was designed specifically for the detention of monks and lamas. An especially desolate area was demarcated for learned scholars, *khenpos, geshes,* and incarnate lamas. Interviewed about this unjust incarceration in such horrible conditions, Adeu Rinpoche responded:

> I spent quite a few years in prison, about twenty altogether. Being imprisoned one is physically unfree; other people decide what you do, where you go, where you sit, etc. Also one's voice is not free, one is not allowed to chant or recite mantras and you cannot say whatever you want. But one's state of mind is not in prison, the Chinese had no idea what I was thinking or imagining. You couldn't

say that the mind was imprisoned in any way whatsoever. I was allowed to remember the Three Jewels, I thought of them as often as I wanted. I was also allowed to remember my own root guru and do any of other practices that I could remember as much as I could. There was nothing the prison guards could do to control that.

But that does not mean that it was not hard. Each morning the guards would dispose of the dead bodies, it could be as high as eighty a day. If twenty people died during the night, we would say it was a good day! Sometimes I would lose heart but then I found it helpful to remember that I wasn't the only one in prison, there were many others too. So there was no use thinking "I am going through a bad time," because so was everyone else, we shared a general karma together. To worry about oneself was like taking on an extra burden that made the whole situation that much more difficult to bear, which was kind of pointless. Later I got released and I had not died.[24]

Rinpoche never had even one speck of resentment in his being or anger in his eyes. The ordeal happened, it was bad, but then it ended.

Seek unerringly a qualified teacher to accept and direct you.

We do not acknowledge or utilize the Buddha nature inherent in our being. Instead, we follow our mistaken perceptions, assuming that all that exists is "out there" and is very solid and real. This duality has created a strong belief in self and *other*; and this is the primary ignorance, which when cleared away causes the collapse of delusion. We need to find a qualified teacher to reintroduce us to our basic nature, guide us along the path, and correct us when we go astray. That we even consider seeking a teacher validates that our inner nature is crying out to initiate transformation. Once we connect with a teacher, we can learn methods to eradicate the erroneous notion of "I" and begin purifying ignorance from its core. All the recitations, meditations, and trainings endeavor to purify that which has veiled us from realizing and stabilizing buddha nature. The teacher, working with you, will determine which approaches and teachings suit your temperament and karmic disposition. A qualified teacher is someone who has overcome all selfish notions, trained on the path to perfection and has fully ripened wisdom and compassion. Conceptual mind cannot fathom nonconceptual wakefulness, which needs to be introduced by someone who is not caught up in dualistic experience: a realized being. In Vajrayana Buddhism, there is no way around the need for a teacher who is the source of confidence in the teachings and the traditional approach to them.

In all nine of the Buddhist vehicles, the key point of the view is emptiness. Each vehicle tries to lead one to the experience of emptiness and to train in it accordingly. Regarding the view, the recognition of buddha nature is paramount. Each vehicle varies in its way of practicing buddha nature. Understanding becomes progressively more refined and closer to intrinsic mind. As Tulku Urgyen Rinpoche notes:

> The teachings are meant to be exactly suited to our
> own disposition and individual capacity. When
> we feel that the teaching fits and that it makes

sense, we can quickly progress training ourselves in it. It is not that the Buddha's teachings differ only because people are different. Teachings suitable to a particular mental capacity were given a certain name among the nine vehicles.[25]

The most important aspect is the correct viewpoint. It is our job to find out exactly what orientation or perspective can truly put an end to ignorance and confusion. "Resolve the nature of your mind; don't resolve the characteristics of all the teachings."

Unlike in the first eight vehicles, the ultimate view in Dzogchen, Mahamudra and Madhyamika is free of conceptual mind. As long as there is conceptual mind, the view is not ultimate. The ultimate view is free of fixation. What it all comes down to is simply how the task of dissolving conceptual mind is approached.[26]

The Path Less Traveled

I confess to not taming my mind.

CONFUSION IS BEWILDERING. I am unable to do anything about this by myself. The perspective of the Buddhist path, simply put, is the effort to clear away this confusion and path here is defined as the confusion of not recognizing the basic state, the ground, to be as it is and mistaking it for something other.*[27] To clarify confusion on the path, I need to study the methods and teachings, I intend to practice, reflect upon them, and undertake their trainings. Through study, I can find ways out of my deluded perceptions, and meet my problems with strength and knowledge. Once I have informed myself of the means, I can apply them, alter my negative habits, and ultimately reunite with the original pure state. Tibetan Buddhism does not ask the follower to give up critical intelligence. On the contrary, it encourages using it in conjunction with the words of the Buddha and enlightened teachers as well as our own personal teachers.

In an age of precision and fine-tuned instruments, we rely on proven resources instead of materials put together hastily. It is vital to apply the same standards for internal work on our fluctuating and unstable minds. The tools with which the Buddha and great masters of the past have endowed us have a twenty-five-hundred-year track record and an undeniable warranty for reliability. They are universally relevant, as opposed to the newest modern techniques that fade as time and consequence pass. The major difference lies in the steadiness of the outcome, which results from the effort and carefulness required in the application of the Buddha's techniques, as opposed to the instantaneous but undependable results promised by New-Age remedies. No matter how archaic and outdated Buddhist practices may appear to be, when put to use, they work.

We need to thoroughly scrutinize the Buddhist methods and figure out if they are suitable for us. A healthy skepticism with honest investigation is highly recommended at this point on the path. Studying becomes essential. That is precisely why, for beginners on the path, it is placed as the first of the three wisdoms (learning, contemplating, and meditating). Do not skip over learning new information and absorbing it in an open and inquisitive way. Never accept any aspect of this training and discipline on blind faith or primitive belief. It is our intelligent responsibility to evaluate what we intend to adopt and practice. As for resources, we have teachers, a breadth of scriptural supports, and current media reserves, both audio and video. Employing these means, we need to compare the information with our innate natural acumen and understanding, questioning the suitability of this way. This basic step is essential; the choices and effort we put into making them are solely our own responsibility.

To be more exact, before committing to any particular contemplative path, apply skillful spirituality shopping. Many cities have spiritual centers or places with bulletin boards teeming with relevant information. You can also find all sorts of events listed in newspapers and community publications. Go to whichever happening attracts you, be proactive and take your time, comparing what is said with your own propensities. Once you touch upon something that interests you, pursue a logically progressive approach to that. Visit Dharma centers and meet study groups; look at the courses they offer there and online, considering each practice and study program with its supportive materials. To help you choose your path, read books related to the tradition you are interested in, whether it be engaged Buddhism, mindfulness meditation, compassion training, nonconceptual meditation or devotional disciplines, to mention a few. I was initially attracted to Zen Practice for its simplicity and directness. I read Suzuki Roshi's *Zen Mind, Beginner's Mind* countless times. Zen was the starting point for me. It taught me how to meditate, though as I explain later in the book, it was more of a passageway than the perfect match. Be discriminating, exacting and diligent and take the time to make the right choice. If you do not live near a center, look at the many wonderful online programs and streamed teachings offered by the Rigpa Dharma Group, Shambhala Centers, Dzogchen Community, Siddhartha's Intent, Mangala Shri Bhuti, Rangjung Yeshe Institute and Nalanda Bodhi, to name a few excellent ones with which I am familiar.

Assimilation of the Dharma into our life commences with these initial stages of study and analysis. Later, we will contemplate this information, and as we become more accustomed and adapted to it, we will develop our understanding through meditation. Applying the Dharma is essential because, unless we bring it into daily life as an integral aspect of our being in whichever ways we are capable, it will remain mere theory. Intellectual analysis, though pertinent and inescapable, will not ignite the alchemical changes that are necessary to attain stability and accomplishment in practice.

First, get the intellectual understanding, next train in what you have understood, and finally attain stability in it by becoming accustomed to the trainings. Learn, contemplate, meditate; habituate them into your being. This is a slow moment by moment process that needs constant nurturing. For me, it is so painfully protracted that sometimes I become discouraged, thinking, "I have done this for so long, why don't I experience any change?" This is especially true when I am overcome by my attachment and anger. Embarrassingly, I don't even think to apply the antidotes in daily life experience that I have been reflecting on while diligently passing time on my meditation cushion. Giving up is not an option then, for sure there will not be any transformation. It is back to the drawing board of practice, again and again.

At such uneasy times I apply self-reflection, which is a recurrent process. I do it whenever the ugly face of ego verification and grandiose importance presents itself, which is quite frequently. I really question why I am so invested in my precise, unyielding point of view to the detriment of the other person, who I experience as an adversary. This dichotomy reveals a hardness that strives to fortify ego clinging and selfishness incessantly with aggressive justification. It does not leave any room for the perceived opponent's inclinations, discontent, and viewpoint. It cares little why the other person is reacting in that specific way and for whichever reasons, or it overrides any consideration of their needs in the push to establish my dominance without the slightest interest to be conciliatory.

If I could just stop at this point and examine my mode of behavior, I would have an opportunity to change and readjust my negative reaction before it becomes out if hand. When I am able, I review the steps I need to take and the Dharma principles I need to apply to transform this situation in a constructive, affirmative way. I accept my own responsibility for the conflict and endeavor to alter any deluded perceptions to reach harmony and agreement and tame my mind.

The temporary negative habits can be cleared away. Dzigar Kongtrul Rinpoche discusses self-reflection as a tool to activate the transformation of habit. As he states, "The study and practice of the Dharma is to really understand one's own habits, to have insight into them from a very clear, objective point of view, and then to find the skillful means to work with these habits."[28] He continues,

We do not have to be controlled by instincts but are able to question these very troublesome impulses. There is the potential to abandon negative mental characteristics and replace them with enlightened qualities. With the support of a perfect teacher and teachings we can study our minds. We can identify that pain and suffering is connected to habits. Habits are linked to disturbing emotions that are bonded to cherishing and protecting the self, which is a product of ignorance.

We can see that directly in our experience. We can discern what is and is not favorable and what does and does not support our happiness. Based on this self-reflection we can gain the courage to overcome all our negative, ignorant traits through the wisdom of the Dharma....

Study the problems first and then make a bridge to the Buddhist practices.... Mind needs to be embraced with wisdom. Give mind something to do opposite to how it normally reacts. Use mind's energy positively; employ wisdom to counteract the habitual power of mind. If you don't do this, habit can get much more explosive and difficult. To outsmart your habits, you have to know them. When you are unaware, habits can control you. If you are aware of them, they have no way to hook you.

Self-reflect on the way your mind is; notice how it functions and how it is dysfunctional.... To progress in this training, pay attention to your

negative patterns and try to get freed from
them. Gain confidence in your positive mental
qualities.[29]

It is important to recognize our actions that are harmful and cause for regret. Once we discover these, we can work to
overcome the tendencies that cause them. Negative emotions lose
their power when we identify them. Being aware is the precursor
to applying the necessary antidote. Dharma works when actualized and we retrain our mind to react in a better way. We need
this self-reflection to root out our hypocrisy. Otherwise, like ordinary people who do not apply any Dharma tools at all, we may
never see our own shortcomings. When such people are angry,
they self-righteously think that it is acceptable to fuel their aggression, rather than correcting it.

Mingyur Rinpoche takes "an objectively scientific perspective, [to determine that] the [Dharma] practices actually
work: feelings of limitation, anxiety, fear, and so on are just so
much neuronal gossip. They are, in essence, habits. And habits
can be unlearned."[30] He explains:

> The brain's active role in the process of percep-
> tion plays a critical part in determining our or-
> dinary state of mind. And this active role opens
> the possibility for those willing to undertake
> certain practices of mental training to gradu-
> ally change long-standing perceptions shaped by
> years of prior conditioning. Through retraining,
> the brain can develop new neuronal connections,
> through which it becomes possible not only to
> transform existing perceptions but also to move
> beyond ordinary mental conditions of anxiety,

helplessness, and pain and toward a more lasting experience of happiness and peace.

This is good news for anyone who feels trapped in ideas about the way life is. Nothing in your experience—your thoughts, feelings, or sensations—is as fixed and unchangeable as it appears. Your perceptions are only crude approximations of the true nature of things.[31]

From my own personal experience of living for thirty years in both a monastery and a nunnery, I do not need scientific investigation and MRI equipment to be convinced of the validity of practice. I have met many extraordinary practitioners, like my main teacher Tulku Urgyen Rinpoche, who exhibited amazing qualities because of his training. Even ordinary young monks and nuns show vast growth over time when they dedicate themselves to the Buddhist path. There is an amazing dignity in simple, experienced meditators, unparalleled by normal people. One of my favorite and most respected examples of this is the grandfather of Tsoknyi and Mingyur Rinpoches, Lama Tashi Dorje. He is a simple unassuming person who has spent his whole life in practice, and is now around ninety-two years old. If you did not already know him, you would never even meet him; he stays in his room and meditates continuously. Only when you go directly before him does his dignity and realization shine forth. He is completely lucid and clear regarding questions about practice, memories of his life, teachers he met, and teachings he received. He is an inspiration for aspiring practitioners and hidden yogis everywhere because he shows that when the words of the enlightened ones strike the flint of diligent experience, the fire of accomplishment blazes.

If you are willing to embark on the path of practice, and train to alter your conditioning, the time has now come to apply the antidotes that transform negative tendencies. Investigating, studying and being honest with ourselves should bring us to the point of committing to whichever transformative discipline we have chosen. Self-reflection and analysis of methods are starting points that prepare the ground for nurturing the process of change. The rest of this book will offer specific Tibetan Buddhist practices and techniques to reprogram our way of looking at and experiencing the world.

Receiving blessing from Tulku Urgyen Rinpoche

With Adeu Rinpoche

Contemplation

I confess to wasting my precious human body.

AFTER STUDYING EACH PRACTICE to be done, I proceed onto the next step, contemplation of the theories. I begin the training in a conjectural, intellectual way. As mentioned in the last chapter, despite applying Zen meditation diligently for seven years, I did not want to continue that practice. I had dabbled in Tibetan Buddhism, but it had not yet grabbed my interest in an authentic way. I did not experience the improvement in my Zen practice that I anticipated. Unable to get direct instructions and answers to practice questions, I decided it was time for a change. Being a somewhat free spirit, doing whatever I wanted, traveling from place to place, like a wandering gypsy, I made the commitment to dedicate the rest of my life to a more serious contemplative existence. I would seek a true teacher and follow his or her teachings and path. My close friend, the performing artist, Bill Fortinbery, was actively involved in a love affair with Milarepa, the great Tibetan mystic and adept. Bill encouraged me to go to Northern India to meet yogis in this lineage who were practicing Milarepa's great tradition of accomplishment. He wrote a letter of introduction to one monastery for me, and guided my decision to go on pilgrimage to India to get the answers I sought.

In my investigation of Tibetan Buddhism, it seemed the total opposite of Zen, which I regarded as simple and fresh. All the bells, drums, deities and mantras of Tibetan Vajrayana practice were a bit daunting and unappealing. Still, I was determined to keep a beginner's mind and search out a Buddhist Master who would accept me in spite of all my reservations about this path. When I landed in Manali, Himachal Pradesh, the humble, realized Gegan[32] Khyentse was teaching a Japanese fellow the preliminary practices, with the aid of a translator, the hidden yogini Ani Jinba. They allowed me to join this cycle of instructions. By this point, I had developed a skeptical attitude toward repeating anything one hundred thousand times, as was required with these preliminary practices. However, the more I listened to Gegan, the more applicable the instructions became. They were completely relevant to my present situation and they made perfect sense. I asked to take refuge in the Buddha, Dharma and the Sangha, did so and made the commitment to begin my preliminary practices in his tradition of Milarepa.

This lineage, the Drukpa Kagyu, is strict, focusing on practice in a step-by-step way. You receive teachings, you practice them, you return to the teacher, and discuss your progress or lack of it. Depending on your results, the teacher gives you the next set of instructions or sends you back to continue on your current one until there are some signs. Gegan was so compassionate, and as simple and direct as a Zen Master, that I persevered in his teachings. I began by contemplating the four thoughts that turn your mind towards the Dharma (also known as the Four Mind Changings). He told me to practice each of the four for a period of four to six weeks. When I finished the time required for these mind changings, I was ready to do anything one hundred thousand times —whatever it took to transcend the sufferings of samsara. I could finally understand the existence of suffering. This is exactly the point of contemplating the Four Mind Changings. When I took them to heart, by going over them repeatedly in my mind, they shifted my perspective at a very deep level; they became valid, understandable and applicable.

The ordinary preliminaries are the teachings on these Four Mind Changings that are simple to understand and unlock access to the Dharma path—without them, I would never have entered the path seriously. These four are the precious human body; death and impermanence; karma, cause, and effect; and the sufferings of samsara. The extraordinary preliminary practices are refuge, developing *bodhichitta,* Vajrasattva visualization and recitation, mandala offering, and guru yoga. I will not go into detail about them here because there are many wonderful instruction manuals that explain much better than I could, such as Patrul Rinpoche's *Words of My Perfect Teacher.*

To have a precious human body is to possess the buddha nature and be free of negative thought patterns that prevent practice of the Dharma in a genuine way.[33] Really contemplate this amazing opportunity, and then look around you. There are so many different beings, yet so few have even the inclination to engage in spiritual endeavors. Just notice your friends and family; typically they are looking for the good life abundant in worldly success and material luxury, most ordinary people pursue comfort for this life and this life only. If they have many things, then they need to get more and protect what they already have. The fear of loss is so strong in whoever has a lot. Mundane people continuously accumulate material objects, not considering the profusion they already possess, and mistakenly believing that these objects will make them happy and fulfilled.

All of us do need to be anxious, because there will be loss. Everything gathered will disperse. All things are impermanent, especially our body, which will one day die. The ever-changing universe does not consist of anything that is permanent and lasting. Everything will disappear like a flash of lightning in the sky. When our life ends, we will be forced to leave behind this cherished body and all the possessions and personal connections we accumulated through so much labor. What does not vanish is the effect of actions, the karmic consequences of our deeds. We will experience these results in future lives when we are born in any of the six realms of existence, where we will suffer the consequences of negative exploits.

Khandro Rinpoche summarizes the four thoughts succinctly:

> You didn't accidentally happen to be a Buddhist or a Vajrayana practitioner. It is the culmination of a million lifetimes of hard work. By not making use of this precious human body, what we are doing is like the example of you being a farmer who works hard, tills and ploughs the land, puts fertilizers, plants the sapling, then looks after it. As the seed sprouts, you tend to it; keep animals from eating it, water it, provide it with sunlight, fence the area around it, and really nurture it. Then the tree grows up, and you are careful with pesticides. You make it healthy; you make it good. It blossoms, has flowers and then fruit. You are sitting under the tree just a day before the fruit ripens to its full sweetness; you pick it and you throw it away to chase a dog. All that hard work gone to waste! We are doing the same thing with this life, wasting it.[34]

These teachings are not imaginary; Adeu Rinpoche said that when he first practiced the Four Mind Changings, he had to enact the six realms in actuality, going through the different experiences of each realm. In our own case, it is necessary that we do not externalize these thoughts as theoretical; they are how each being undergoes reality in actuality. We may be skeptical of the existence of the hells and hungry ghost realms, but it is easy to find the tendencies for these places in our own stream of being.

Take anger, for example: observe how we can blaze with the self-righteousness of the hot hells, and become internally preoccupied and consumed with the intensity of aggression. Anger perpetuates itself by identification with the emotion. Haven't we heard people say things like "I was so angry that I saw red"? The flames of the hells are also the metaphor for being so consumed by hatred that our emotional environment is only one of pain. There is also the total isolation and defensiveness of the cold, steely anger that separates us from other people, as if in an icy environment like the cold hells. The freezing winds of selfishness and aloofness fracture us, yet haven't we repeatedly justified such feelings, along with our greed and stinginess.

We callously roam around over-satiated and anxious to procure more and more without regard to sharing or being generous. It is as if we are making reservations for the hungry ghost realm. Don't we experience stupidity and unawareness? We are often as dull as animals. Consider how animals actually live, either in constant fear of being killed or as mute slaves subject to the whims of their owners. With strong attachment, humans always try to manipulate reality to create personal happiness. Don't we abandon the wishes of other people when they interfere with what we perceive to be best for us? With jealousy akin to the realm of jealous gods, we see everyone as competition and we lose the ability to rejoice in the success of even our friends. Our pride is the sure setup for the abandonment of and downfall from the state of grace. Endlessly distracted, we wile away our time like the gods.

Certainly, we hold ourselves above our concern for others. Such behavior is a vivid reminder of each of the six realms brought into our present situation. Repeatedly, we relinquish altruism in favor of what is most comfortable for "me." We need to admit our own proclivity for these experiences. All these realms "exist" due to our deluded perceptions. However, the precious-ness of the human realm is that it provides the best body to enable us to connect with the innate nature. There is the opportunity to tap into the most vital of qualities. It is said, "When obscurations are removed, realization occurs spontaneously."

Tulku Urgyen Rinpoche best sums up the necessity of training in the Four Mind Changings:

> When the mind is totally stripped of obscura-
> tions, realization is like a wide-open, clear sky
> with nothing to obscure it in any way whatso-
> ever. A famous quote says, once you have taken
> the four mind-changings to heart, you will have
> formed a solid foundation and Dharma practice
> will not be at all difficult. If not, it is like trying
> to build a house without a foundation. But sim-
> ply having repeated the mantras and having the
> idea, "Okay, I did it," will not be the foundation
> for higher practices.
>
> Whatever is built upon a solid foundation, will
> be like the stories of a building that will remain
> firmly grounded and stable. It's not enough to
> strive for the higher teachings and ignore the
> real substance of the Dharma, which is a change
> in attitude. Unless we can change our hearts at
> a deep and profound level, the samsaric traits of
> our personality will all remain, and we will still
> be seduced by appearances. As long as our mind
> is fickle, it is easy to become carried away in the
> chase of power and wealth or the pursuit of beau-
> tiful objects, in concerns of business and politics,

in intrigues and deceit. It is easy to become an insensitive practitioner who cannot be "cured" or changed by the Dharma. Although one may have great theoretical understanding, it does not penetrate to the core. That state is like a Tibetan butter skin, which is the container for the butter inside that is not made flexible by the butter itself, even though the skin holds the butter.[35]

With the Four Mind Changings, now is the time to embark on formal contemplative training. When beginning contemplative training, time and place are crucial. Find an area of your living quarters to denote as sacred, your shrine. Arrange a comfortable seat or chair as your meditation cushion. A place near a window is favorable—clean, open, and fresh. The most important point is to keep a straight back when in session, because when the back is straight, the channels inside the body are straight, and then *pranas,* the breath, can move freely. By not being tense and constricted, you lessen the tendency to create inconsequential thoughts.

Sit down, relax your body and mind, and begin the contemplations on the Four Mind Changings, starting with the precious human body. Numerous guidance manuals give details about how to engage in this training.[36] Choose one of them and read from it before or during your session as a support. Finally, arrange a regular time each day for this practice and be consistent with this as well as with the length of time spent in contemplation. Do not break the continuity.

We have been introduced to the concept that we are essentially perfect and pure, but right now, it hasn't really helped us that much. Obscured by ignorance, we are unable to receive the manifold benefits inherent in our perfect and pure nature.

Not recognizing this basic ground, the original state is shielded from us. We need to apply various techniques to cleanse our habitual tendencies and reconnect with our original state. The Four Mind Changings are some of the powerful cleansing agents that we should apply daily.

Tulku Urgyen Rinpoche

Tsoknyi and Mingyur Rinpoches and their mother

The Teacher Component

I confess to doubting the need for a teacher.

GOING FOR REFUGE is the entrance to the Dharma. We place our trust in the Buddha as exemplified by our teacher; the Dharma, the teachings; and the Sangha, the noble companions on this path. When taking refuge, it is important that you do not view your teacher as ordinary, but as a sublime being whom you have the rare opportunity to study with and serve. In the practice of refuge, we seek protection from conditioned existence. We visualize our teacher in the form of a fully realized buddha—Padmasambhava, Tara, or whomever we feel a strong connection to. Our whole environment shifts into a buddha field and we begin the process of reconnecting with the vast clarity we have lost.

Taking refuge is the way to connect with actualizing the great purity and equality, as Dzongsar Khyentse Rinpoche explains:

> Devotion is integral to being a Vajrayana practitioner. Wanting to be free of delusion implies accepting that we are deluded. If we never abandon our impure ordinary perceptions of the mundane world and lives, we will never break out of our delusion....
>
> Usually when we take refuge, there's a sense of being lower than the object of refuge. You, a pathetic being, need to be saved, and you take ref-

uge in this very wholesome, omnipotent being.
Refuge could feel like that, but if you understand
the great vastness, then, you will know we are
not separate at all. Think that your guru is a reflection of your own buddha nature. It actually
makes you familiar with this idea of the great purity and equality, which is the whole purpose. It's
really incredibly important....

There is a beautiful composition by Jigmey Lingpa, a song of Calling the Guru, invoking the guru
from the heart, which clearly elucidates that the
guru is not an ordinary human being out there,
nor is the guru someone who is going to dictate
how you should live your life. It's not like that
at all.

It is a very beautiful and poetic metaphor: The
guru dwells within your own heart. This is totally
different from our ordinary perception, whereby
we think that the guru is external and separate
from us. The heart refers to the buddha nature.
As one of the infinite manifestations of the buddha nature, there is faith, and as a reflection of
this, devotion. When devoted people see through
the devotion manifested from their buddha nature, they see their guru or spiritual companion.

Please, never forget that in all the Vajrayana
practices, one always merges with the guru and
becomes indivisible. This is called receiving the
empowerment or initiation from the guru.[37]

No matter which discipline we follow, we need someone who knows more than us to show us the way, whether that person is a trainer or a teacher. Since we do not experience our own inherent purity, we cannot fully appreciate the purity of others and the world. A realized teacher has gained certainty and stability in his or her basic nature. He or she is able to transmit that understanding skillfully and compassionately to the student. Once we connect with a wisdom teacher, it is crucial to accept that we are unrealized and that our teacher is not. Such openness and appreciation has immeasurable value.

The different trainings we undergo make our minds more pliable and receptive, but they do not completely set us free—that is only accomplished through recognition, training, and attaining stability in mind nature. The best-proven method for introduction to mind nature is by our teacher, a living realized being who also corrects us when we go astray. This vibrant and indispensable relationship is crucial for progress on the path. Vajrayana offers full accomplishment in one lifetime and in one body, however, to commit to Vajrayana necessitates relying on a true spiritual guide. There is no way around this requirement. The most direct way to connect with our inner qualities is to find a skilled teacher and request teachings. Our link with our teacher is the most significant and important connection we will ever have with anyone. The root teacher is the person who points out the nature of mind. When mind nature is pointed out and recognized, it is as if Buddhahood is placed in the palm of your hand.

Introduction to and recognition of mind nature both arise from openness and love for the teacher. The moment of that love frees us from conceptual thinking; that very openness is the gap that allows us to awaken to our inherent nature. Trust in the teacher and teachings is a type of love that strips our mind of its normal tendencies. We can stop calculating and dissecting each

moment and break free of all obsessions. As Tulku Thondup
notes, "Devotion is one way we have of letting go of the idea of
self. Belief helps us to open. It is the releasing of doubts and fears.
Being open and receptive is a way of asking for the help we need.
This is a simple way of surrendering self. It acknowledges the belief that grasping and trying to control everything leads us away
from wisdom."[38]

With Tulku Urgyen Rinpoche, I had many opportunities to
confirm this premise. I often practice outside when training in
mind nature. In keeping to my gurus' instructions and the guidance manuals, I take up various activities to enhance practice. For
me, dancing is one of those exercises that augment clarity. It is
also a way to be free from my standardized self-image, since so
much of my perceived identity is projected when I dance in pub-
lic. I question how I look, how good a dancer I am, and so on. Directing myself away from self-consciousness is a joyful release.

One cloudy day when I was dancing around outside, a strong
feeling of compassion welled up in me for the many unhappy beings who lack the opportunity to meet with these trainings. At
that very moment, the clouds opened up and a clear blue sky
burst forth with the warmth of the shining sun, and I was filled
with love and appreciation for Dharma practice. Later in an in-
terview with Rinpoche, his response to my question described
exactly that experience in detail. It was an incredible affirmation
for me that he had not only acknowledged what I had undergone
in such a skillful way but that he utilized it to guide me further.
My mind was stripped bare of ordinary thought, and my trust in
him deepened.

The obvious question that arises is, if there is the tendency to
misapprehend, how can we be sure that we will make the right
choice in deciding upon a teacher? It is up to us to investigate
different teachers thoroughly until we meet one who inspires us,
and in whom we can develop trust. The wish to look for a teacher

comes from our hidden buddha nature, which is calling out to us from within in the subtlest way. Our buddha nature is encouraging us to seek fulfillment beyond the normal constraints of modern materialism. It generates the yearning to return to basic mental and emotional healthiness, to be liberated from negative states and develop into our full potential.

A true teacher is the culmination of all the past teachers in his or her lineage. Pure lineage in Tibetan Buddhism is traceable and identifiable. It is proven by historical figures and realized masters to this day. We can trust the Buddha; he got it right and produced a definitive map to enlightenment. Each qualified teacher carries an unbroken transmission of this plan.

Take the time and energy to scrutinize which teacher and system speaks to your spiritual objectives. Don't commit immediately, first be skeptical before committing. Your teacher will become the most significant person in your life. You don't want to rush in and find out later that you were mistaken. Once you do entrust yourself to a teacher, according to the Vajrayana, a complex new set of rules will apply. Transgressing them will have serious repercussions.

You need to use your discriminating intelligence to check out any teacher and teaching with a highly critical mind. It is much better to step away before bonding and acknowledge your mistake. There are definitely fake gurus and manipulative, badly motivated people around. Beware! As Jigmey Lingpa has said, "One has to learn how to examine the guru, how to examine the path, and how to examine the methods." We do so by studying and reflecting upon the teachings. Examine, be suspicious, and mull over in your mind what the right teacher and teachings would be. When you are sure, do make the commitment. To paraphrase the Buddha, "Do not take my teachings at face value. Examine them, as you would inspect gold you intend to purchase. First determine if it is pure and authentic, and then make the deal."

My root teacher, Tulku Urgyen Rinpoche, exemplified everything for me: my teacher, my best friend, my father, my child, and the love of my life. He never disappointed me, deceived, manipulated, or misled me. He was a combination of full realization and political savvy. He was attentive to the tiniest detail, and he never rescinded his promises. He was consistent in every situation—giving teachings and empowerments, catching a train in Paris, or close to death in a Taiwanese intensive care unit. I stayed with him personally for seventeen years, and I never saw him give up on a single individual. One day my partner and I scolded him for not disciplining one of his out-of-control students whom we considered dreadful. He responded that he just didn't see people as bad. He never allowed anyone to break a sacred pledge with him.

Other minor examples of his skill in guiding students can be found in his teaching style. It was said that the Buddha could give teachings to a large assembly of disciples and, due to his power of perfected speech, each individual would hear the teachings in his or her own language. A master like Tulku Urgyen Rinpoche manifested this quality in a different way. For years, Rinpoche had audiences with his Western students in the evening in his tiny room at the top of Nagi Nunnery. It felt cozy to be in such intimate surroundings and circumstances with Rinpoche. He sat in his box-bed and all of us squeezed together with the cockroaches running around on the table in front of us. He would begin the session by asking if anyone had any questions, which of course we all did. Someone from overseas would probably get to ask first. The answer would go on for about one or two hours depending on Rinpoche's health and whether or not his attendants interfered. When Rinpoche had finished and requested additional questions, it always happened that during the course of the teaching, everyone's questions had somehow or another been answered. He knew each mind without having to be told. This happened time and time again.

Rinpoche did not know more than a few words of English, yet when the translator stopped, he would begin, extraordinarily, with the piece that the translator had left out. Tulku Urgyen Rinpoche taught in accordance with the needs of his students. For example, if you were a Dzogchen practitioner, he taught you Dzogchen; if you were a Mahamudra practitioner, he taught you from a Mahamudra context, without having to be informed of your allegiance in either case. Whichever path you followed, he could touch the essence of your training. Once, a student brought his brother John, a Zen follower, to receive teachings from Rinpoche. After leaving the room, John stated, "I don't know what you all are talking about, Zen being different from what you learn. The teachings I just received are the same as the most brilliant discourse I have ever heard from the most advanced Zen teacher." Rinpoche had taught him in the manner of a Zen master.

Tulku Urgyen Rinpoche did not experience time in the linear way that most of us do. He gave me a teaching one January using a very obscure example. Twelve months later, he continued on, further elucidating the topic at the point he had left off at the beginning of the year, stating, "As I was saying the other day." Of course, such qualities are not unique to Tulku Urgyen Rinpoche, and are shared by other realized masters as well. I often compile books from transcripts of audio recordings, checking the Tibetan teaching against the English text. I compiled one book, *The Songs of Naropa* by Khenchen Thrangu Rinpoche, from two successive years of teachings on the same topic. In addition to Thrangu Rinpoche's lucid explanation, it was impressive that he did not duplicate anything from one year to the next. To my utter amazement, in a way similar to Tulku Urgyen Rinpoche, he mentioned a point in the second year that he had previously touched on in the first year, and carried on from where he had left off.

Without a teacher, it is impossible to attain realization of the ultimate view of the Great Perfection or Dzogchen. We need to receive the blessings of a genuine teacher to recognize our buddha nature. People might believe that they can discern absolute truth through studying books and going to lectures. These can provide a theoretical understanding, but the true nature of emptiness is beyond ordinary thought; thinking cannot access it. That is the primary reason to obtain advice and teachings from a qualified teacher. Every buddha in the past relied upon a teacher. Through devotion, beyond ordinary dualistic mind, we can acknowledge the absolute truth, our buddha nature.

To reiterate, we have the opportunity to break away from the conceptual chains that bind us. It takes more than sheer intellectual analysis to step out of normal constricting patterns. Devotion is the way to strip off rational servitude. Simply being in the presence of realized masters and observing them is a transforming experience. As Patrul Rinpoche said, "In particular, the authentic realization of the natural state cannot but be accomplished by extraordinary faith and pure perception toward those spiritually more mature than yourself, and extraordinary love and compassion for those who are less so."[39]

This line of reasoning is contrary to the empirical scientific methods to which we are accustomed. We have learned to accept materially present and solidly substantial realities as truth. We are instructed to doubt any experience of intangible energies, such as the blessings of a realized teacher and the state of enlightenment itself. Science is limited to techniques and equipment that can prove theories within the domain of mundane mental cognitions. As the equipment gets more sophisticated and the hypotheses more complex, last year's established suppositions become obsolete. With internal, spiritual, or mental science, we are asked to reverse the process —to trust the immaterial and question the material.

People often ask me who my teacher is now that Tulku Urgyen Rinpoche passed away. I reply that, "My teacher is Tulku

Urgyen Rinpoche." My connection to him is through practicing the teachings he gave me as often as I can throughout my waking hours. He and his teachings are a constant source of support, inspiration, and connectedness. I do not feel separate from him when I train. Of course, I miss the physical presence, the smile and the voice with the heart advice that was accessible to me in all situations, whether difficult or joyous. However, Rinpoche left me with the greatest legacy that a revered and cherished person could bestow: the instructions for the path to enlightenment.

I am fortunate to be one of Tulku Urgyen Rinpoche's biographers and archivists. He entrusted me with many of his audio and video recordings, which I have made available as much as possible. Working with this material has been a renewable gift that never ceases to amaze me. I have been able to observe retrospectively that from the onset of his teaching me, he laid out the road map of how he wanted me to practice through the course of my life. As my familiarity with the path deepens, my understanding of his methods becomes that much more profound. Rinpoche had an overview that extended way beyond the years we were physically together. I increasingly appreciate his compassion, generosity, and brilliance and laugh with him whenever I listen to his teachings as audio files.

I take support from other teachers as well, and seek out clarification from the many wonderful masters alive today. I believe that I need to check my understanding and conduct with the guidance of realized beings. I need to continually break apart my confused preconceptions and receive explanations. Even though a teacher is not my root guru, these many wonderful guides are my teachers for different practices. I seek out students of Tulku Urgyen Rinpoche or accomplished masters who teach in a similar way. This prevents my practice from drying up and becoming stale. Don't we all need this renewal from time to time?

Bodhichitta

I confess to transgressing my bodhisattva promise.

ONCE WE HAVE TAKEN THE REFUGE PRECEPT, we avoid the ten negative actions of body, speech, and mind and adopt their opposite, the ten virtuous actions.[40] Most basically, never even consider harming another sentient being. The Mahayana trainings are expressed by the superior attitude that combines compassion with the view of emptiness. This cultivates the mind set on supreme enlightenment. This topic includes the relative bodhichitta of aspiration and application and the absolute bodhichitta: "The bodhichitta of aspiration has two aspects, compassion, which is directed toward beings and wisdom, which is directed toward enlightenment. Neither aspect by itself expresses bodhichitta. If you do not aim at attaining ultimate enlightenment, then however strong your wish to benefit beings may be, you will never go beyond ordinary kindness and compassion. If you wish to attain enlightenment for your own sake, you will never go beyond the limited nirvana of Hinayana practitioners. Both aspects are essential."[41]

Before I explain further, I would like to tell a story of my own experience with these practices that illustrates how profound they are and how they work when applied. Towards the end of Tulku Urgyen Rinpoche's life, many distasteful events transpired among his close disciples, Western students, ordained nun attendants, and the major Karma Kagyü lineage holders. It was a dark time, as if we were riding a derailed train speeding down an embankment and waiting for the impending crash. Among the Western students an ugly rift developed that dramatically played out for two years. It was an extremely painful, stressful time and not how one would wish to remember the final years of one's guru's life. A European student headed one flank in the battle, opposed by a few others and myself. I felt strongly that the European student, who had assumed control of Rinpoche's medical care, was damaging Rinpoche's health, thereby shortening his life. To protect Rinpoche from harm, I secretly entertained the idea of making my nemesis permanently disappear.

How did I come to be willing to abandon the most basic Buddhist principle of not harming another sentient being, not to mention the secular morality that prohibits killing? It is not a short or easy story to tell. It came about only after the buildup of negative perceptions over many years, and reached a culmination during Tulku Urgyen Rinpoche's subsequent illness. However, any number of experiences that diverted my mind away from its ability to handle conflicting emotions cannot serve to justify my failure.

We each bring to our practice a set of conditioned realities and past karmas that we cannot openly see. Many who choose the Dharma path do so out of severe pain and frustration that are not expressed in their lives. As I mentioned, in my own case, my feelings of uneasiness and not belonging propelled me to seek a sacred path. It is impossible to know what deep wounds others might harbor, and I cannot judge their situation. I can only convey my own lack of insight or ability to deal with negative circumstances. Instead of looking at myself closely and discerning my inability to apply the teachings in a suitable manner, I judged harshly the behavior of another. From the other person's perspective, he may have been convinced that he, like me, was acting out of pure intention for the greater good. Without deep self-analysis and reflection, Dharma practice can become just another patch to hide under and avoid our real issues.

In this case, I certainly did not view the other person as acting benevolently, nor did I utilize the skillful means of the path. At some stage during Rinpoche's final years, an unspoken power struggle developed over access to him and control over what he could teach and to whom. This contest mingled with the medical care that Rinpoche required. In charge of that area, someone could manage contact with the guru. Instead of having the most highly skilled, compassionate professionals be in charge of his treatment, it became a political tool that was tightly orchestrated through self-interest by most of his caregivers. Naturally, as Rinpoche aged, he became progressively weaker. He was afflicted with several serious diseases, high blood pressure, diabetes, and angina. Each health crisis precipitated even tighter monitoring by those who had taken authority.

The atmosphere around the lama in the last years was maintained by the threat of violence against anyone who disagreed with the status quo. Not even Rinpoche's sons dared interfere. Rinpoche was fully aware of what was going on. His primary intention was to protect all of us from ourselves. There were to be no confrontations, no exposure of wrongdoings, and no blame. Rinpoche wanted all to maintain their sacred commitments and keep connected to the Dharma and to him. He stated that he did not want anyone to leave Nagi Nunnery, since he had only a few years left to live. If such bodhisattva activity necessitated that he offered up his life, then so be it. I, on the other hand, was not willing or ready to let Rinpoche make that sacrifice. I suffered in the abject horror that to continue the current course of medical treatment would prematurely end Rinpoche's life. Unfortunately, I was completely helpless to change the direction of where this was leading. I developed a distraught and vulnerable mood that entertained murder in order to halt the inevitable.

I had lost the ability to view all of this as my own deluded phenomena and karmic situation. My mind became enmeshed in

circumstantial conditions, and my course of action became a per-
verted projection of my personal, limited agenda. I was unwill-
ing to be open to the teaching Rinpoche was giving. If Rinpoche
wanted to protect this person, who was I to harm him?

To mentally compensate for my wrong view I tried to
draw a parallel between my position to that of a past life of the
Buddha, when he was a bodhisattva-captain on a boat with five
hundred other bodhisattvas and one evil man who planned to kill
them all. Through his clairvoyance, the bodhisattva-captain knew
this man's intention and could see the incredibly bad karmic ripening and immeasurable suffering the evildoer would undergo
upon carrying out his plan. The bodhisattva-captain killed the
evil man to prevent him from accruing that karma and harming
so many noble beings.

Justifying my thoughts, I took a similar line of reasoning.
I considered the consequences, and compared the damage the European student was doing against such a heinous act as homicide.
I investigated the possibility of locating a contract killer. To my
surprise, it was relatively easy and amazingly cheap, if I used local
talent, and more expensive and risky if I hired foreigners to do
the job abroad. In retrospect, I was astoundingly arrogant even to
consider that I had the same powers of judgment as the bodhisattva-captain. My level of distress adversely affected my basic intelligence, so that I thought I could karmically handle the conscious
act of intentionally harming another being. Fortunately, when I
shared my plan with a close Dharma friend, he talked me out of
it. He convinced me that whenever I got another human rebirth,
after lifetimes in the lower realms, probably my enemy would
be born as my child. I knew as well that such a negative action
would greatly displease Rinpoche, since there was nothing even
close to being virtuous in such monstrous thoughts.

The story of the bodhisattva-captain who killed the evildoer is told to illustrate the fact that bodhisattvas will sometimes

work contrary to seven of the ten virtuous actions for the ultimate benefit of the other person. However, they do so out of incredible wisdom and compassion devoid of even a hair tip of self-interest and ego clinging. They also undergo suffering voluntarily as the result—the bodhisattva-captain was reborn in hell. Intending to kill someone and still act in accordance with the Dharma supposes that you have the power to liberate them and send their consciousness to a pure land, as exhibited by several *siddhas* like Tilopa. Unless one has this power, killing is murder, which is the result of being deluded and misguided:

> Enemies are the projections of our own deluded mind. As long as we mistakenly perpetuate the belief in subject and object—the objects being whatever is perceived and the subject being the dualistic mind that perceives something as being "other" than itself—then there will always appear someone or something "out there," which is perceived as harming "me." This is nothing other than a projection produced by clinging to duality. This projection of duality is the real enemy.
>
> You will create tremendous negative karma if you cultivate the idea that there is someone "out there" who is your enemy and who should be killed so that he is unable to harm you. Killing the enemy is only half of it—it is possible to destroy your enemy—but to guide that consciousness to the pure lands is much more difficult. It is our projections that need to be killed.[42]

Not seeing the other person as dear and precious, I broke my bodhisattva vow. After giving up the idea of killing him, I had exhausted all avenues of warfare. The situation escalated until Rinpoche passed away. It was only then that I found out how to subdue my enemy. Instead of destroying him, since no amount of aggression had worked, I decided to apply the bodhisattva trainings of loving-kindness and compassion. I conscientiously worked with my mind, applying the practice of sending and receiving in a very concerted effort. Sending and receiving, or *tonglen* in Tibetan, is a practice that coordinates breath and visualization. With the exhalation of breath, you send out all your happiness, love, and good fortune to sentient beings; with the inhalation, you receive all their misfortune and sufferings. I imagined my enemy in front of me and exchanged my contentment for his conflicted state of mind. I sincerely wished him unchanging joy, peace, and happiness. Then whenever I actually met him, I treated him with openness and genuinely felt warmth. The transformation was almost automatic. He changed how he reacted to me as well. Since the object of competitiveness was gone and my hatred dispelled, he could accept the tenderness and sincere caring. This reversal of attitude and its positive result incontestably showed me how powerful the Dharma is when its skillful methods are used appropriately.

This episode also exposed my instability. I become confused when trying to interpret and apply the teachings in difficult situations. I saw how I spend a lot of time going through the motions of practice and not really taking the most basic teachings to heart. I hadn't worked directly enough with self-serving emotions. Continuing like this will inhibit the necessary changes in kindness and compassion from truly manifesting. The Dharma works when correctly applied, as this story also illustrates. The texts and the teachers list the signs of correct learning and practice, which include being more gentle, finding it easier to cut off negative emotions while increasing trust and compassion. I wish

I could say after all these years that I exhibited these qualities, but I don't. At least I am not too jaded—I still shock and disappoint myself with my bad behavior. I continuously make the strong determination to improve. Misusing the Dharma to harm others will turn out as Gampopa warns: "When the Dharma is not practiced correctly, it is the cause for going to the lower realms."

> *If I do not examine my own defects,*
> *Though outwardly a Dharma practitioner, I may act*
>   *contrary to the Dharma.*
> *Therefore continuously to examine my own faults*
> *And give them up is the practice of a bodhisattva.*[43]

I have another unusual confirmation of bodhichitta practice in the story of a mentally unstable old nun of Nagi Nunnery. Maya had been diagnosed as manic-depressive and was on medication. Over the twenty-four years I lived next door to her, I witnessed times when she went off her medication and experienced outrageous episodes that resulted in her hospitalization. She had a good heart and was kind and funny, but she did not seem able to do any Dharma practice. When she died, the lamas thought that they should dispose of her corpse as quickly as possible, and they arranged for the cremation within twelve hours of her death. However, it didn't happen that way, because she sat in *samadhi,* or meditative composure, for the entire next day, in a state called *tukdam* in Tibetan. The signs of tukdam are that the heart remains warm, rigor mortis does not set in, and the body does not begin to deteriorate or smell. The whole atmosphere around a practitioner who stays in tukdam is serene and inspiring. It was exactly like this in our neighborhood. The power of Maya's good heart overrode all the difficult circumstances of her mental illness and medication. What a supreme validation of bodhichitta!

Apply the practices of relative bodhichitta in aspiration and application with the objective of relieving all beings of their anguish. Engender the good heart and infuse it with loving-kindness and compassion in thought and action. Enhance relative bodhichitta by making the wish to attain enlightenment to benefit all beings. By recognizing and stabilizing the view of emptiness, train your mind in absolute bodhichitta. Embrace the view of emptiness. Once enlightened, we will be capable of leading others to enlightenment, bringing them definitive happiness and the perfect causes for that.

Right now, uproot all clinging to the self as primary. To help others, and establish them in uncommon happiness, we need to perfect and integrate the authentic teachings with our mind and enact them through our conduct. As Dzigar Kongtrul Rinpoche instructs,

> Our tendency to cherish the self, protect the self and be exclusively focused on the self can be changed with a simple and effective method. We remove our self as the focus of cherishing and protection and replace the self with others. When you do this, you're not getting rid of cherishing. You're not getting rid of protecting—just changing the focus from our self and putting others first. The new cherishing is developed through logic and reasoning. . . .
>
> Now the focus is on directing the same feelings, the same emotions, not on our self, but outward. Cherish others as we cherish ourselves, protect others as we protect ourselves, and by using our tendency, our loving-kindness and compassion will increase. . . .

We learn how to cultivate happiness through loving kindness, compassion, sympathetic joy, and equanimity. We cultivate an altruistic mind, the wish to benefit all beings, to bring them to a perfect state of happiness and the causes and conditions of that, and to perfect the state of freedom from suffering and the causes and conditions of that. Training in all of these is the increasing of relative happiness inside our mind. . . .

We do this by suppressing the old habits of ego and then training in generosity, discipline, patience, diligence, meditation and wisdom.[44]

Train in a way similar to the contemplations on the Four Mind Changings. Make the determination to practice, and set aside the time and place to do so. Begin by sitting in a composed way on a comfortable seat. Settle your mind in a relaxed manner and start to contemplate the Four Immeasurables. These are loving-kindness, wishing all beings to be happy and have the causes for happiness; compassion, wishing that they be free from suffering and the causes of suffering; sympathetic joy, wishing that they not be separated from happiness; and the attitude of impartiality, wishing all beings to benefit equally from these. Long for all beings to be happy and freed from their afflictions. Hope that they never part from true happiness. Say:

> *May all beings possess happiness*
> *May they be freed from their suffering,*
> *May they never part from the happiness devoid of misery,*
> *And may they abide in impartiality, the equal nature of all*
>   *things.*[45]

It is not complicated to engender unequivocal, sincere compassion for countless beings. Think of all those who suffer in natural disasters, earthquakes, wildfires, floods, epidemics, and so on. The loss of life and property compounded by the anxiety of separation from loved ones is overwhelming for both humans and animals. Think about AIDS patients dying alone in hospitals, and the elderly who linger listlessly in nursing homes, wishing they could die. Remember the child soldiers whose youth has been ripped away by conflicts and wars, and the innumerable women raped and sold into the slavery of the sex trade. Such abuse is incalculable.

Now, think of yourself, sitting comfortably on your meditation cushion and the wonderful circumstances and causes that placed you there. This culmination of good fortune is such a blessing, that we merit such freedom, and are able to practice the genuine Dharma and strive to benefit these beings. At this point, exchange your pleasant, serene state of mind with the angst and pain of these other fearful, desperate beings. Breathe in their misery and send out your happiness with your breath; this is tonglen, the exchanging of oneself with others.

Experience the suffering. Bring it clearly to mind and exchange your well-being and positive energy for their fragile, uneasy mental states. Wish lovingly to establish all beings in everlasting contentment; not in the normal samsaric happiness, but in the true happiness of living and acting in accordance with the Dharma, when one engages in virtuous activities of body, speech, and mind. Rejoice in the good fortune of all those noble beings who have traversed this path and those who are now journeying on it.

Another way of looking at rejoicing is "practicing so that your own mind doesn't cave in to despair, envy, or jealousy."[46] Try to benefit impartially the many beings that need our prayers and affirmative wishes. "As time goes on, you will see how those heart-felt feelings that are extended to others cleanse, secure and bring your mind to another level of happiness."[47]

By training in relative bodhichitta, we restrain our normal dualistic tendency to cherish ourselves above all others and we act upon that intention and aspiration by taking the six *paramitas*—generosity, discipline, patience, diligence, meditative concentration, and wisdom—as our applied conduct. We act generously to less fortunate beings. We conscientiously apply practice instructions daily. We hold back from aggression and retaliation. We attentively adopt virtue, and meditate on the nonexistence of self and phenomena. We apply our natural intelligence, endowed with spiritual wisdom, as much as possible.

At this point, it is important to mention a teaching called the Three Excellences, which should be carried out in any practice session. Tulku Urgyen Rinpoche describes these as follows:

> The first, the excellent preparation of bodhichitta, is compassion. Begin with [refuge] and bodhichitta, then move on to the main part, [whichever practice you are doing] and end with the excellent conclusion of dedication, which is also bodhichitta, the dedication of merit for all sentient beings.
>
> If there is not this prayer for beings, then there is a split between buddhas and beings. Compassion is the connection between buddhas and beings, which sticks them together, the glue that binds. It is not like buddhas go off to be content by themselves, "Oh now I am a buddha, I'll close the door over there." Just joking, but really there is no selfish work. There is one Eastern Tibetan proverb for this: "Self-benefit is finished for a

buddha. All dualistic fixation is purified and they only work for the benefit of others." It is by this power that later, countless emanations for the benefit of beings will appear without having to think, "I want to act for the welfare of beings. I am going to emanate." There is no need for such concepts because the state of buddhahood is free from concepts. This buddha activity appears through the power of karma and aspirations like a reflection in a mirror. It is the effortless welfare for beings.[48]

Our intention to connect with and benefit beings is a heart-felt prayer that will come to fruition the more we train and transform ourselves. Aspiration puts us in the ranks of "people of noble birth and family," the dignified company of those who, according to the Buddha, have engendered the good heart and given birth to the Dharma in their being. As Khenpo Kunzang Pelden explains in his commentary on Shantideva's *Bodhicharyavatara:*

It does not matter whether they are men or women, young or old or whether their position in society is high or low. If the jewel of bodhichitta arises in the minds of sentient beings, they instantly undergo a change of identity. Henceforth, they are crowned with the name "Child of the Sugatas." They are called Bodhisattvas, heroes and heroines of enlightenment. Their status changes: they become objects of reverence and offering of the whole world, both gods and human beings. They are, moreover, said to be worthy of reverence even by the Buddhas themselves, for the latter have bodhichitta as their master.[49]

Meditation

I confess not seeing my mind as the Buddha.

MEDITATION IS TO ENCOUNTER YOURSELF without any bells and whistles. It is working with your mind directly, stripping it bare and naked in a gentle, nonthreatening way. Trungpa Rinpoche writes, " [Meditation] is the means of rediscovering ourselves and our basic goodness, the means to tune ourselves into genuine reality, without any preconceptions or preoccupations."[50]

As mentioned briefly before, I lived for some years of my youth in a hippie commune. After I left there, I worked on thoroughbred racetracks in Kentucky, Florida and California. It was seasonal work, moving from meet to meet and various horse sales. The transient lifestyle suited my gypsy nature. In between the hippie commune and racetracks, I decided to learn how to meditate according to traditional methods, having foregone some more far-fetched techniques. I received my first instructions at the Zen Center in San Francisco from Kwong Roshi, a gentle teacher to whom I am greatly indebted and whom I never met again. I practiced diligently every day without cutting the continuity. I went to the Zen Center at Green Gulch whenever I had the opportunity, and read and reread *Zen Mind, Beginners Mind* innumerable times. The whole time I worked with horses, I continued to practice meditation on and off the track. Riding on the racetrack and breaking and training "babies" on the farm taught me a one-pointed presence of mind and body: distraction caused accident and injury. Several years later, I heard Trungpa Rinpoche quoted as saying that the saddle was a substitute for the *zafu,* the meditation cushion. That coincided with and affirmed my own experience; to be a good rider or a good meditator you need concentration that is not too loose and not too tight.

There came a time when, as a meditation student, I felt that I needed direct, insightful, personal instructions and clarifications that were not readily available to my situation. I decided to go to Asia to meet Tibetan lamas and find my teacher. First I met Gegan Khyentse and shortly after that I was fortunate enough to meet Tulku Urgyen Rinpoche. I have followed the guidance he bestowed upon me with varying degrees of diligence ever since. Meditation trainings are diverse and wide-ranging: what suits one person may not work for another, and so much is dependent upon one's disposition and past karma. A skilled teacher will be able to determine what will work best for each student. Meditation, like all other aspects of Tibetan Buddhist practice, cannot be learned solely through books. I can paint a picture for you of what it might be like, but you need to take the opportunity to find resourceful and proper guidance, through personal contact with a meditation teacher.

There are two primary ways of approaching meditation: through the analytical style of a scholar, or by means of the resting meditation of a simple practitioner. Whichever manner you prefer once again depends on your propensities. There are, however, some basic principles of how mind functions that do not differ, which I touched upon earlier and will explicate here. Mind, in this context, is defined as being awake and conscious. Thus, thoughts such as anger, and perceptions such as mental images and memories are identified as the expressions of mind. We associate "I" with mind, the truly existing self who thinks, feels, and acts. Mind is actually a continuum of many instances of recollection that happen so quickly we think they are uninterrupted. In fact, they last a fraction of a moment to the next fraction of a moment, with a short gap in between as each moment rises and ceases.

It is this uninterrupted chain of thoughts and perceptions that accumulates karma. Meditation can break that sequence and strip away the layers that prevent us from experiencing our true nature. However, "the ultimate view is recognized by being introduced through direct personal experience without being dependent on analysis through philosophical speculation or exerting yourself through techniques."[51]

We have now been informed repeatedly that everything is a projection of a mind that does not truly exist in either an outer or inner way. Let's study how mind functions and see if we can gain a simple understanding of its workings, and then begin to apply meditation techniques to reprogram the normal tendencies. Analytical meditation is a series of investigative questions about the identity of mind, thought, and perception. The meditation progresses through first examining mind, its origination, abiding place, and disappearance, as well as its shape, color, and definable characteristics, and so on. After reaching experiential confidence about the lack of any of the above, the student moves onto thoughts and perceptions, scrutinizing these in a similar way. This methodology is undertaken in all three of the great views of Tibetan Buddhism—Dzogchen, Mahamudra, and Madhyamika. This training challenges many of our preconceptions concerning mind, thoughts, and perceptions.[52]

It might be easier to accept the nonexistence of mind, thoughts, and perceptions than that of outer objects, so let's look at this next. When we see an object, e.g. a cup, we first react by acknowledging exactly what it is. After that, we give it labels: "This is a good cup," for attachment; "This is an ugly cup," for aversion; or no opinion about the cup at all, for indifference. Tulku Urgyen Rinpoche comments, "We are all alike in this respect: when we see something beautiful, we like it, something ugly we dislike it, and something neutral we don't care about it. Those three basic negative emotions manifest in relation to our five senses and the outer sense objects. The subject, our mind within, likes pleasure, dislikes pain, and can also remain indifferent. These six types of experience—visual form, sound, smell, taste, texture, and mental objects—are called the six collections of consciousness."[53] Thrangu Rinpoche explains this whole process extremely clearly:

> The mind experiences the world through the five senses. However, our mind consciousness itself does not experience sights, smells, sounds, tastes or textures directly. What is being perceived is a mental impression of these experiences. Based on that mental image, we create secondary thoughts about past, present, and future. We determine what we like and don't like, what should be accepted or rejected. That activity is named the sixth consciousness.
>
> We tend to believe that this perceived object is somewhere outside and the perceiver, the mind, is considered to be somewhere inside. All perceptions, be they the objects of the six consciousnesses or all the different thoughts and emotional reactions that might arise, are not external to us; they are mental occurrences that take place in our mind. Therefore, all things are our own mind. Believing objects to be external is a mistaken concept.
>
> The seventh aspect of consciousness is called "disturbed mind consciousness," and is something that is ongoing. It is definitely a quality of ego clinging, but is not as pronounced in the way of the thought "I am" as is the sixth consciousness.

Rather, the disturbed mind consciousness is like a subtle background noise, an ongoing feeling of holding onto itself. This is present in every situation, whether we are awake or asleep.

The eighth is called the "all-ground consciousness," or the alaya-vijnana in Sanskrit. It is also a type of background consciousness in the sense that it is the ongoing clarity or the conscious quality of mind. The alaya is what allows for any experience to take place, whether there is or isn't any thought involvement, whether or not we are interpreting the input that is presented through the senses. The quality of being able to cognize, to be awake, aware, and so forth, is something that is steady and continuous. Through all our beginningless lifetimes, this all-ground consciousness has been the basis for the habitual tendencies that recreate the different ways we perceive things. This is why it is called the all-ground consciousness.

It is the mind consciousness, the sixth aspect, which refers to that which thinks that practices meditation. We see sights, and notice various sounds, smells, tastes and textures. Accompanying those experiences is an act of conceptualizing, which attaches labels and values to what is perceived. It's the mind consciousness, which associates judgments with these sense impressions and it is conceptual.

This mind consciousness does not perceive objects directly. The sixth consciousness apprehends a "mental image." This mental image is presented in our mind and is then fused together with all sorts of different associations—for instance the name of the particular object. Let's take the example of a pillar; the sixth consciousness will create the idea of "pillar" by fusing together a conglomeration of various impressions based on all of one's past memories about different pillars. These are put together in one generic image that we connect with the word pillar. The sixth consciousness associates and identifies a certain sense imprint—what is simply presented through the senses—as being a pillar. This is different from the visual cognition, which is simply a direct sense impression of what is present. Sense cognition does not attach any labels or values—it is non-conceptual. It is the mind consciousness that starts to classify and define the current image. Through this process it creates an idea and some structure as to what it is we perceive. It culls memories from the past and premonitions of the future, melts these together with many other things and labels that mix with the name "pillar." So, among the eight consciousnesses, only the mind consciousness meditates. In other words, it is the thinker who cultivates the meditation state.[54]

Normally the sixth consciousness, our mental consciousness, looks away from itself, seeking gratification in outer, perceived objects. Through the practice of meditation, this process is reversed, and the mental consciousness comes back inward and looks at itself. Now, gleaning some basic understanding of the workings of mind, let's begin with a primary form of meditation: *shamatha* or calm-abiding meditation. The classic example given to describe the reasons and benefits of this practice is looking in a pond of water and wanting to view your face. If the water is stirred up and murky, you cannot see it, but if the water is clear and still, the reflection appears unobstructed. The first step in being able to distinguish our natural face, buddha nature, is to calm down the rush hour of thoughts and anxieties that drive us ceaselessly, day and night, and bewilder the mirror of our mind until it is unavailable and concealed. Right now, we are not working with pure phenomena to change our unstable and volatile minds—that comes later. Instead, we begin by reuniting with the most basic element in our makeup—our present awareness— through posture, mindfulness, and breath.

As in earlier trainings with the Four Mind Changings and bodhichitta, assume a comfortable seat in your sacred space. A relevant but rarely acknowledged point is that meditators should wear loose-fitting clothing that doesn't constrict body or breathing in any way. It is helpful to place your meditation cushion on top of a yoga mat or a larger cotton one of dimensions suitable for sitting on the floor, because for some it can be cold or uncomfortable, and thus distracting, to have legs directly touching the hard floor or ground.

Sit cross-legged or with your right leg slightly extended, whichever feels correct and relaxed. The most important, essential point is to keep your back straight; if you need to sit in chair, please do so. Your hands can be placed in several ways: either the position of ease of the great adept Longchen Rabjam, hands resting on the knees; or you can place your left hand lightly in your right one with your thumbs touching ever so gently at your navel, as if holding a piece of paper between them. Keep your head and neck straight, with your eyes fully open, gazing downward toward your nose; this naturally makes the eyes half-closed. In later meditations, there will be instructions for looking straight ahead in midair, but for now that might make it more difficult to steady the mind.

Your breathing should be normal and regular, not forced or contrived in any way whatsoever. Particularly, according to the Dzogchen tradition, breathe through the mouth, not the nose. To start with, merely count the inhalation and exhalation of the breath from one to ten. While you inhale and exhale, count one as freely as possible. Don't do anything else with your body, speech, or mind. Simply concentrate on your breathing. If you observe your mind wandering, bring it back to the inhalation and exhalation of the breath. Sessions should be short but of good quality, and you should extend them as you gain confidence.

All meditators immediately notice a deluge of thoughts and feelings, and some think that it is the meditation bringing these up. It is not—it is only that you were never aware of them before. This undercurrent has been running incessantly and ceaselessly through your mind-stream day and night, and only now do you become conscious of it. This is what calm-abiding meditation will bring under your control. Congratulations, you have taken the first steps to mastery of your mind! As mentioned earlier, whenever you are doing virtuous activities, it is indispensable to encapsulate them within the Three Excellences. Begin with the excellent preparation, the wish to benefit all sentient beings, bodhichitta; engage in the main part, which is here the meditation; and conclude with the excellent dedication of merit.

Shamatha is divided into several categories, primarily with and without object or support for the attention. As this training has many divisions and a progression in techniques, it is best to be under the guidance of your teacher or a meditation instructor. For example, once you perfect the supported shamatha with a reference point, next you practice unsupported shamatha without a reference point. This also has many key points and methods to train in before moving on to the next meditation, vipashyana.

To become accustomed to these types of meditations, as outlined above, seek an instructor to help you progress on the path. At some point when you feel comfortable and want to enhance the practice, an outstanding method is to go to an open place with a wide, vast vista. Sit there outside on a crisp day, in either the early morning or late afternoon, when there are no clouds in the sky and it is crystal clear. For some people it is occasionally helpful to practice near a body of water, either by the gentle flow of a creek or river or the vastness of the ocean. If the sun is directly overhead or in front of you, it will be uncomfortable. The spot should be warm, fresh, and clean, with an unimpeded view. Sit so that the sun is at your back at either of these two times of day. If this is not possible, have the sun to the side and wear a hat with a wide brim.

Begin as usual with the refuge and bodhichitta verses, and then engage in shamatha with a reference point. After some time, abandon the method, directing your gaze to the space in front of you. Do not outwardly solidify the openness or stare vacantly; instead, with awareness, mingle your vision with the unobstructed quality of the sky. Keep mindful that you do not become lost or absorbed in the space, or lose the alertness of the experience. Whenever you notice that you are being carried away, return to a mindfulness in which you do not follow after thoughts of the past, present, or future. If you find yourself becoming dull or scattered, break up the session. Meditate in short sessions of high quality, bright and awake, repeated often to sustain the freshness. Dedicate the merit when finished.

When ending a meditation session, Padmasambhava teaches, "End the session while still at ease—never while uncomfortable. Do not end the session while unclear or during thought movements but while experiencing clarity and nonthought. Then you will not tire of the meditation training. Ending the session while it is good causes one to later joyfully take up the practice again, and it also ensures that the qualities will continue to develop in your stream-of-being."[55]

Healing with Tara

*I confess to accepting and rejecting in regards to
the deity.*

ONE OF THE FIRST SETS of instructions and empowerments that I received from Tulku Urgyen Rinpoche was the
Tara practice based on several hidden treasure texts revealed by
Chokgyur Lingpa, entitled *The Essential Instruction of the Three-
fold Excellence* and the *Zabtik Cycle*.[56] Tulku Urgyen Rinpoche's
style and emphasis was on recognizing mind nature and mingling that with all aspects of training. Later, I was fortunate
enough to receive more elaborate and detailed explanations on
this same cycle from Adeu Rinpoche. I would like to take this
opportunity to recapitulate and review these instructions, offering them as an inspiration for physical and emotional healing
for oneself and others.

Up to this point, we have not linked to a deity. The pure,
transcendent energy in our practice has come by way of blessings
from our teacher and the power of his or her wisdom mind mingled with our devotion. Here we connect with the sublime phenomena of a pure wisdom deity by the power of skillful means,
our resolve, and openness. To practice deity yoga in a detailed and
perfect way, it is necessary to receive teachings, reading transmission, and empowerment from a qualified lineage holder. I will be
merely the medium for you to know what to request.

Taking the support of an unadulterated, blessed entity
and being influenced by it has healing and regenerative qualities.
Through dedication and sincere prayers, combined with the wis-

dom and power of the sacred object—the Buddha, for example—we can overcome obstacles and gather advantageous circumstances to rekindle the recognition of our inherent nature.

Tara is an especially strong resource, because innumerable people have relied upon her practice to receive benefits and spiritual accomplishments for well over two thousand years. The stories most often associated with Tara describe how she pacifies and overcomes all fears and dangers for those who venerate her.[57] She is known as a source of supreme knowledge and healing. She is a fully enlightened buddha in female form. As Orgyen Topgyal Rinpoche describes,

> Buddha Shakyamuni himself, when teaching on Tara, said that among all the other buddhas, Manjushri and Tara are the two who have exceedingly great resolve. Tara is an emanation of the mother of all the buddhas of the three times. She carries out all their activities, dispelling the obstacles created through the eight or sixteen types of fear. Most significantly, she vowed to emanate in female form until all of samsara is emptied. When anyone supplicates Tara, her response is swift. The activities resulting from her aspiration are extraordinary, and there is ample evidence of this, right up to the present day.[58]

It is vitally important to rely on a spiritual symbol of enlightenment to maintain mindfulness, clear away hindrances, and imbibe blessings. Deity practice is a gift that we develop and take support from until we ourselves embody the deity's remarkable uniqueness. By doing this, we acknowledge that we can awaken our inner potential by seeking help from a seemingly outer source. Traditionally, deity yoga includes the practices of development and completion stages that employ the visualization of the deity's body, the recitation of its mantra or speech, and the samadhi or concentration linked to its mind. These trainings purify that which prevents us from recognizing and sustaining the natural state by making our minds pliable and less fixated on solid, coarse reality. We are trying to affect the immaterial by connecting with pure phenomena that have a transformative power. The profound methods of devotion to and pure perception of an enlightened being can become an alchemical component of change for the benefit of oneself and others. Please note that the principles outlined here can apply to any other realized being besides Tara, such as the Buddha, Padmasambhava, Longchenpa, or your own root teacher.

In this context, I need to mention another significant point: how things truly are and how they appear or manifest. Tulku Urgyen Rinpoche explains, "According to the sutra system, one talks about the relative and ultimate truth, but in the Great Perfection teachings one talks about the way it is and the way it appears."[59] Adeu Rinpoche puts it this way:

> The expansive wisdom mind is identical in all the buddhas. Out of this, they manifest various forms to benefit beings with individual proclivities and dispositions. The special quality of Tara is her extraordinary compassionate resolve to benefit all beings by removing whatever causes them to feel anxious or afraid, and dispelling the eight or sixteen types of fears.
>
> There are two perspectives: One is that Tara was a practitioner on the path who first developed the wish for ultimate supreme enlightenment, progressed on the path, and finally awakened to

buddhahood; another is that Avalokiteshvara's tears turned into Tara. How does one reconcile these two versions? That depends on the capacity of whoever is listening to the teachings. For ordinary people, the perspective of someone like oneself who progresses along the path is presented. Yet, the true perspective is that in the Akanishtha Buddha Field, all buddhas awaken to enlightenment, and then their emanation is seen as if attaining enlightenment in a world of ordinary beings. In actuality, there is no real conflict here between the two versions of the story. One is the relative perspective—you might say the superficial version—while the second is the ultimate, real perspective.[60]

Shamatha with Tara as a Support

Tara is a refuge against obstacles, an inspiration to all impoverished individuals, and an enabler of the manifold enlightened activities of buddhas and bodhisattvas. Praying to her and performing her practice brings swift results through the link to the power of her potent aspirations. From within the perspective of shamatha, where concentration was on the breath, now take Tara as support.

When using Tara as a support, place a Tara statue, painting, or photo in front of you. Look at the representation, study it, memorize the details, and close your eyes, keeping the image in mind and vividly recollecting the characteristics. Gaze again at the likeness and repeat, closing and opening your eyes until you can mentally recreate the image. Next, project that reflection into the space in front of you. Visualize Tara, seated upon a green lotus and moon disc, as the vibrant, sparkling, emerald green buddha that she is, evanescent and shimmering with a body composed of light. She is peacefully smiling, sitting cross-legged with her right leg slightly extended. Her right hand is at her knee in the gesture of giving, in which the fingers point downward with the palm facing forward. Her left arm is raised to the level of her heart center in the gesture of granting protection, the palm forward and fingers pointing upwards. Between her ring finger and thumb she holds the stem of an *utpala,* a fully blooming blue lotus, with the blossom at the level of her ear. Her hair is partially tied up with billowing silk streamers in a crown jewel, and the rest of her hair is free-flowing. She is adorned with different jewelry, earrings, short and long necklaces, bracelets, armlets, anklets, and a jeweled belt. She wears silken garments, which include a shawl, sash, skirt, and leggings.

When you feel carried away and diverted by thoughts, bring your attention back to the mental image of Tara. Sometimes close your eyes for a few moments and regain the image of Tara; then reopen your eyes and remain free. If very agitated, lower your gaze, and if extremely dull, raise your gaze upwards towards Tara's eyes. If neither state is perceptible, simply keep the awareness at Tara's heart center. Adeu Rinpoche advises,

> Jamgön Kongtrül explains that you simply use this specific practice as a support for capturing the attention. Do not worry whether the image is vivid or dull, precise or vague, whether the mind rests or does not rest, and so forth. You should completely abandon any such hope, fear, worry or concern. Simply keep mindfulness on guard against getting distracted and wandering off. . . .

By training in this repeatedly, the attention eventually is captured. When it has been caught, you
simply remain there, undistracted, very relaxed
and natural, for as long as you can sustain it. At
the end of the session, imagine that the form of
the deity before you melts into light and is absorbed into you, so that Tara's mind and your
own mind are indivisibly of one taste, and then
remain in equanimity.[61]

Shamatha without Support

After you feel confident in being able to keep your attention on Tara as the object of nondistraction that steadies your
mind, you can progress on to the next type of shamatha: unsupported, objectless shamatha. Raise your gaze and place it gently in
midair, looking at the space directly in front of you. Do not rely
on your breath or hold any image as a reference point for your
concentration. Instead, initiate loosening up your mental focus.
Simply allow your mind to rest naturally in open space. When
thoughts occur, do not follow after them. Merely acknowledge
their arising and let them fade.

Depending upon our physical constitution and different
situations, dullness or agitation might overcome us. When dull,
raise your gaze, open a window, or remove some clothing. When
agitated, lower your gaze and exhale. Consciously try to regain
your composure, stabilizing your mind, and then continue.

When you feel somewhat even, rest with the eyes looking smoothly into space, somewhere in the middle of the low and
high perspectives. Adeu Rinpoche counsels, "Usually in this kind
of practice you go back and forth between being focused and
being relaxed. There is some fluctuation between these. As you

grow more accustomed, you do not fluctuate too much between being too concentrated or too tight and too loose. You cultivate a more balanced way of sustaining awareness."⁶² These meditation methods lay the groundwork for progressing on to *vipashyana* meditation training, which I will not address in the main body of this book. For more information on this topic, please look at appendix 1.

Tara as a Method for Healing

Now, we will proceed to practicing with Tara as a means of healing yourself and others. Even on the mundane level, it is widely agreed that a positive mental outlook can have positive consequences, especially to transform illness and unhappiness into better physical and mental health. By relying on the means of Vajrayana as a conduit, we can connect with the sublime positive energy of enlightened beings.

How often have we found ourselves in the situation where someone close to us is having a hard time and we feel powerless to lessen his or her distress? Whether it is illness, having been violated, undergoing death, or the death of a loved one, we can lessen their suffering by practicing Tara on their behalf. By sincerely supplicating Tara with them in mind, we can help diminish their fears, anxieties, and dilemmas.

Once again, visualize Tara in the sky in front of you as described earlier in shamatha with an object. This time, don't apply any specific concentration to control your mind as done in shamatha. Instead, begin with the consideration that such a fully enlightened being has inconceivable qualities that promote nurturing and healing. Please understand that deities are all identical in essence, and that by accomplishing one deity, you accomplish them all. It is only in our ever-discriminating minds, that some deities represent certain areas of influence and capability. Tara happens to be connected with protection and the fulfillment of positive activities. She epitomizes the vast array of qualities of the enlightened state, and by relying on her as an exceptional model, we approach these divine characteristics ourselves.

Start by instantaneously imagining Tara vividly in the sky in front. Tara is pictured as brilliant, emerald green, sparkling, evanescent, and intangible, like the rainbow after a storm clears the air of mist and clouds. She has an ephemeral body of light overflowing with warmth and radiant qualities. If you are unable to get a sharp depiction, just relax into the tenderness of her loving-kindness and compassion. The feeling of the deity's presence is the most important aspect. Sense that she is nearby, and bathes you in her wisdom, kindness, beauty, and care. She is present the moment you turn your attention to her and are open and devoted.

Recite the lines of refuge from appendix 2 or simply develop confidence that Tara is present. Generate bodhichitta, thinking that you are practicing to benefit all beings with the particular troubled person in the forefront of your mind. As you repeat the words three times, with the thought of Tara present, keep generating positive thoughts for all.

After that, imagine that you transform into Tara. Embody her qualities, and determine to be an intermediary for healing and regeneration. All of these concepts are your mind. Your mind creates the representation in the sky before you, forms the thought of yourself as deity, and makes the aspiration to help others. Your mind is insubstantial and nonconcrete, but awake and aware, the unity of being empty and cognizant.

What is pictured in the sky in front is the deity of your own concentration and trust. Due to your openness and love combined with Tara's aspirations to benefit all who call upon her, she appears as the wisdom deity, who melts into your visualized one like water poured into water. Rest for a few moments having the assurance that Tara has heard your prayer and has arrived.

With devotion, recite the "Homage in Twenty-one Verses" in appendix 2 or merely hold the image of Tara in front of you with tenderness. When reciting, say the praise slowly, bringing the meaning to mind. Maintain the mental picture of Tara in your presence to the best of your ability. It is good if you can say the mandala offering prayer, also in appendix 2, before the twenty-one praises. If this is too complicated in the beginning, hold off and be conscious of the praises themselves.

When you reach the second repetition of the praises, direct your attention to Tara's right hand. Once pointing downward in the gesture of supreme giving, it now shifts to point upward, with palm still facing out, as it changes into the gesture of offering refuge. Imagine that you and the person you are practicing for (envisioned sitting next to you) come under her protection. You are both firmly within her sphere of influence. Once again, recite the liturgy and, if possible, the lines of mandala offering before reciting the praises. At the very least, make sure to read the lines that describe the movement of her hand.

By the third recitation of the praises, having read the lines for the mandala offering and the subsequent visualization, you are ready to engage in your objective of healing and assisting. From the body of Tara, white light flows out like liquid and enters the crown of your head and the crown of the head of the person in need. The stream of nectar purifies all negativity, illness, unhappiness, and fear. It is a rejuvenating, blessed elixir that dispels any obstructions and unpleasantness. Now focus on the purification and healing aspect of the practice. If you want to repeat the twenty-one praises, do so as many times as you feel comfortable.

After this, with full confidence that you have accomplished your aim to nurture, protect, and cure, allow the front

visualization to dissolve into you. Without the slightest hesitation, you become Noble Tara. In that state, recite the ten-syllable
mantra, either the Tibetan pronunciation, OM TARE TUTTARE TURE
SOHA,or the Sanskrit OM TARE TUTTARE TURE SVAHA.

After chanting this a convenient number of times, end
your session by bringing about the self-assurance that your mind
and the mind of Tara are inseparable. Remain for as long as you
can in awareness, free of thoughts. Conclude by reading the lines
of dedication for the benefit of all beings and in particular for
the person of your concern. You can also bring his or her name
to mind in a special inclusion during the dedication, mentioning
their name aloud: "for all beings and especially _____.

The more often that you repeat this practice, the easier
it becomes. As you begin to feel more confident with it and less
overwhelmed, you can add the other twenty Taras into your front
visualization. They are similar to the main figure, but are of different colors and have various emblems. In the beginning, it is
all right to concentrate on the single figure and not overextend
yourself with too much detail.

We might doubt whether, at our level of realization, we
can be of assistance to anyone. We cannot give the ultimate benefit that leads beings to enlightenment, but temporarily, by practicing correctly, we can definitely help. When I once asked Tulku
Urgyen Rinpoche about any effects of my current practice, his
response was,

> It is not that one has or doesn't have power; it
> is not like that, because you are not relying on
> yourself in this case, you are relying on deity,
> mantra and samadhi, which is where the power
> lies. This practice has the power to liberate all
> sentient beings. Combining the sincere wish to

purify beings disturbing emotions and establish them in the ultimate state of enlightenment while reciting the mantra and training in the state of samadhi, meditative concentration, is the means for accomplishing benefit, there is the power.

Moreover, compassion benefits others, especially if we combine compassion with the view of emptiness. We don't assist them directly, like by giving food or clothing, but emptiness and compassion purify their misdeeds and obscurations. Some people say, "Compassion is pointless. We want something to eat or wear that would be sufficient. What is the use of merely wishing others happiness and benefit?" Yet to think, "May others be benefited with the combination of emptiness and compassion," is best, because to have compassion is virtuous even though it does not help in a physical manner. However, sentient beings do have misdeeds and obscurations, and to wish, "May their misdeeds and obscurations be purified," will essentially help against those misdeeds and obscurations.

If with a very pure heart you dedicate the merit to other sentient beings in the long run that will help them, it will create the link that can truly benefit others. Just giving food and clothes actually, of course will temporarily help a little bit but it doesn't effect on any deep level. If you connect that with the dedication and aspiration for sure that purifies the obscurations of other sentient

beings. The thought, "May all material and immaterial virtue benefit all sentient beings," then
you have both dedication and aspiration.[63]

Please also understand that, as Tulku Thondup Rinpoche
notes, "Relying on external healing sources is helpful and even essential as long as we are under the control of dualistic concepts
and depend on external objects. However, it is important to understand that the ultimate healing is going beyond dependence
on external forces."[64]

Tara as a Guru Yoga Practice

Another supreme way to purify our negative habits,
uneasiness, and despair is to engage in the guru yoga practice,
which ordinarily comes as the final section of the preliminaries. It is the openness and love of devotion to a sublime being or
an accomplished teacher that brings forth realization, as well as
purification, positive conditions, and the dispelling of obstructions. Regarding the teacher not as an ordinary person but as a
fully enlightened being brings us closer to the Vajrayana view of
all-encompassing purity, and guides us toward tapping into that
source of perfection.

Here visualize your guru in the form of Noble Tara in
the sky in front of you. After taking refuge and generating the
enlightened resolve of bodhichitta, chant the twenty-one praises
once followed by the ten-syllable mantra of Tara. During the recitation, really yearn to embody the qualities of such a benevolent,
omniscient buddha in a way that will benefit not only you, but a
countless number of suffering beings. At the end of the recitation,
envisage that from Tara's forehead a white light radiates downward and touches your head; from her throat center a red light

radiates downward and touches your throat; and from her heart a dark blue light radiates downward and touches your heart. Finally, from all three places combined, rainbow rays of light radiate and dissolve into you. Think that these lights purify your ordinary body, speech, and mind and that you obtain the blessings or empowerments of enlightened body, speech, and mind and their combination.

At the end of the session, Tara melts into light and dissolves into you. Tara's body, speech, and mind mingle inseparably with your body, speech, and mind. Remain in that state of indivisibility as long as you can. When finished, dedicate the merit. By training in this way, we purify our strongly solidified tendencies of self and other, subject and object fixation, and grasping mind. We are utilizing the subtle to loosen our coarse predetermination of reality as solid and truly existing. In so doing, we begin to lighten and remove these stains.

Conduct

I confess to losing the conduct in the view.

So OFTEN, I FEEL THE NEED to control what is happening around me and keep it orderly and structured. This would be an extremely precarious situation anywhere, but especially when living in a country like Nepal, where everything is random, explosive, or uncertain at best. For example, after ten years of civil unrest has impeded upkeep and development, we face a lack of electricity. Residents must contend with subsequent load shedding, in which electricity is turned off for certain times of the day. The electric company publishes its schedule periodically, but keeps to that timetable for a few days, before arbitrarily changing it at their whim. This lack of predictability is more disruptive than losing electricity for sixteen hours a day. Given my personality, if I knew in advance, I think I could plan for it

Trying to determine the future is an illusion, because nothing in cyclic existence is definite or predetermined; everything is subject to change and uncertainty. Most of us want to be able to plan and arrange our lives in a convenient, methodical fashion, only to face disappointment. Since all is constantly in flux, no one can hold on to the present moment: it is fleeting and insubstantial. Yet, even knowing this, we try to control events and establish some kind of permanent happiness. The powerlessness that underlies most experience produces a subtle, persistent uneasiness. We anesthetize ourselves against this knowledge, reassuring our ego that we can make that appointment for next

Thursday beyond a shadow of a doubt. All the while, we are approaching death, which definitely comes without an appointment or a plan.

The upheaval these unsolicited transformations cause reveals to me how unstable my mind is. I become overly obsessed with keeping everything carefully arranged in a place where nothing works out that way, yet I still try to convince myself it can. When my presence of mind returns, I try to relax into light-heartedly letting go of preconceptions. Once I get over the fact that change will haphazardly undermine my plans, I can appreciate what a great teaching change provides. How can I possibly expect to face all the challenges of dying and death if I do not have any real control over my mind? I waste so much time in endless preparations—do I have time to die in the middle of all my plans? Will I be able to schedule death in my calendar of events, since it is the only certainty I unequivocally face?

By treasuring each moment of awareness in the face of the inevitable end, preparing for death prepares us for life. Behaving in accordance with this authentic foreknowledge infuses us with great caution about karma and its result. We do not need to wait to practice. We must consider that we could die at any moment, and stop procrastinating and giving the excuse that we are waiting for all the right conditions to come together: a comfortable place with a great view and stylish interior, a support staff, a financial nest egg, and all the teachings lined up with the teacher close by. We cannot continuously let the time slip by because this situation doesn't happen. We could get sick, a family member might need us, or some calamity might waylay us.

Shifting our priorities with death in mind motivates us to engage seriously in the Dharma practice, which could greatly enhance our lives. We need to periodically investigate and reflect upon the results of our practice, and ascertain how the teachings are internally embodied. Diligently applying the practices of accumulating mantra numbers and cushion time is indispensable, because it brings us closer to actualizing the view, but most notably we need to exhibit the result of all this effort in our conduct. In our daily lives, we need the different methods and trainings to habituate us to become conscientious. To have a superb intellectual understanding of the view is not good enough. Rather, the view needs to be actualized so that it sustains us through challenges and becomes an intermediary in all our actions. Without close introspection and self-evaluation, we might convince ourselves of progress when in fact there is none. We need to set the highest standards for ourselves and transform anything negative in us into a positive state. Khandro Rinpoche advises:

> To discover absolute truth, first ready the vessel of our mind—and that begins with genuine honesty. It is an honesty that one doesn't have to speak to somebody else and therefore can be surprisingly naked without any political niceties, etiquettes, or protocols, something you come face to face with. Eventually this is the ground that you are going to have to work with.
>
> Ask yourself, "How much a sensibility have I developed and courage in being able to let go of forms of practices so that the heart can be a kinder heart? How much kindness have I cultivated? How much transition and transformation has come about through my recitations and meditation and the learning of Dharma? How much change in my mind has come about in extending unbiased compassion towards all sentient beings?" In checking and examining within yourself, if you really find some work done in

making it a kinder heart, then that is a very fortunate practitioner. At the moment of death there
will be absolutely no regret knowing that you did
exert effort in the right direction.

Being a Buddhist is to be one who develops the
mindfulness of abandoning all the hindrances
that impede genuine kindness, where your devotion, your effort, your different aspects of practices, methods, form and formless meditations,
and the limitless number of teachings that you
have received allow you to develop a strength-
ened mindfulness that precedes all actions of
body, speech, and mind, and transforms them
from being unvirtuous to virtue. Such a person
can then refer to him or herself confidently as a
meditator, as a yogi, as a true practitioner.

That is what being a Buddhist meditator is about.
If that is not being practiced then it is rather an
interesting long journey, but other than it becoming a preoccupation and busyness unfortunately
not much can be gained from it. Not to fall into
that is one's own responsibility. Each teacher
and teaching you practice basically says the same
thing again and again. Therefore it is essential
to realize the profundity in the teachings and to
cultivate that in your actions.[65]

Ultimately, we are our own quintessential judges; we
may deceive and manipulate other people, but we should not de-
lude and lie to ourselves. We have to ascertain where we have
honestly come to on this path. Are we taking the precious teach-

ings deeply to heart, or are we merely using them as a gloss or an additional set of vocabulary by which to hide our negativity and impress others. I have encountered some scenarios when people use Dharma terminology like "my intention is pure," while all the while the toxicity of their motives isn't even lightly veiled. Although intention cannot be viewed materially, eventually hypocrisy becomes difficult to hide. As Trungpa Rinpoche notes, "There are two extremes: one extreme is indulgence in the intellectual sense and in intellectual discovery, the other extreme is using the impulsive, instinctual level of the ego as camouflage to prove your state of mind in terms of the teachings."[66]

Conduct includes what should be adopted and what should be avoided. Our conduct should embody the highest standards of virtue. We should recognize that worldly pursuits are insubstantial and will not bring ultimate happiness to anyone. Habituated to meaningless action, we neglect the sublime path of accomplishing Dharma that is the only refuge and achievement of consequence. Instead, we circle continuously in conditioned existence. Moreover, we should conduct ourselves in accordance with the specific Dharma teaching that we are practicing. As Adeu Rinpoche remarks,

> We attain certainty by means of the view, practice by means of the meditation, bring forth enhancement by means of the conduct, and arrive at realization by means of the fruition. Conduct is how a meditator behaves as their practice progresses. There are various types of conduct. In the beginning, it is essential to follow the Mahayana ideal of the bodhisattva, behaving in accordance with the six paramitas. These are different forms of behavior, but the important thing is that we should act in accordance with our view so that

our behavior and mode of conduct can assist and
help deepen realization of the view; otherwise it
can be rather risky and dangerous.

Padmasambhava said, "Do not lose the conduct
in the view; rather be brave in the view and timid
in your conduct." If you lose the conduct in the
view then you can easily stray into "deluded dis-
sipation," a continual stream of delusion, thinking that it is a high view. On the other hand, if
your conduct is quite high but view is not, then
you will merely be acting like a highly realized
yogi, rather than truly being one; this will not
work either. Turning one's stream of being into a
continuous flow of delusion is not going to work.
Brave in the view means willing to recognize the
highest view of Dzogchen, but not act accordingly in all one's behavior. One should still respect
the fine details of cause and effect and be aware
that one's actions do have consequences.[67]

Tulku Urgyen Rinpoche had total confidence in our ability to recognize, train in, and attain stability in mind nature. He
encouraged us to combine it with all activities. When close to
him, I felt positive enthusiasm and conviction radiate out from
his experience and realization that was contagious. He made it
seem so easy and completely natural to train in recognizing mind
nature. He continually encouraged his students to practice in that
style. I trusted him and endeavored to do so, but in one exchange,
I did air some of my doubts to him. I asked, "Rinpoche, what if
you have not correctly recognized mind nature and train in an
intellectually fabricated state and then abandon purifying obscurations and accumulating merit through conventional practices?

Won't you be doing nothing but deluding yourself? Isn't it better for beginners like me to be on the safe side and practice both with and without concepts, accumulating merit and wisdom simultaneously?" He had to laugh and agree that incorrect recognition is useless.

Losing the conduct in the view occurs when practitioners like me over-exaggerate our realization of emptiness in our actions, and lose sight of the limited ability of others to allow experiences to "self-arise and self-liberate." I may firmly, and perhaps mistakenly, believe that I have such an ability, but I need to be cautious not to antagonize or upset others. Sudden emotional outbursts do leave a karmic imprint on people that may liberate for us but not for them. It is as Padmasambhava said, "Though your view is higher than the sky, keep your deeds finer than barley flour." Tulku Urgyen Rinpoche comments on this famous line:

> Understand the expression "finer than barley flour" to mean to adopt what is virtuous and avoid what is evil, with respect for the law of cause and effect, with attention to the smallest detail. This is to keep harmony between view and conduct. The opposite, separating one's actions from the view, is to somehow convince oneself that there is no need to do the preliminary practices; no need for any good deeds; no need for making offerings, and no need to apologize for evil actions. One can fool oneself into believing one need only remain in simplicity. What this honestly means, though, is that such a person will have no spiritual progress. Ultimately, it is definitely true that there is nothing to do, but this is true only after one has passed through to the other side of understanding, experience, and

realization. To maintain an intellectual conviction of the view without having undergone the
training is a severe misunderstanding. This is
how the self-professed "Dzogchen practitioner"
goes astray.[68]

It is said that receiving praise can be one of the biggest
obstacles, for that is when we can fall prey to Mara, the great
demon. We may end up overestimating ourselves and believe
our progress to be better than it is, and therefore not apply that
much effort. Sickness and unhappiness are much stronger spurs
to practice than happy times are. It is much better to be slandered
and criticized than praised, for at least we can discern whether
the disparagement is true or not, whereas compliments subtly undermine our progress. When blamed and accused, we are forced
to evaluate the causes and conditions that have led to the situation and to investigate our own responsibility for it. Whether
completely valid or not, it is definitely the ripening of some past
karma. We should apply ourselves to generating the virtue to
overcome these impediments.

Some Dharma practitioners decide, before they reach the
shore of nonthought suffused with wisdom and compassion, that
they can assume crazy-yogic behavior. They say and do whatever
they feel is appropriate for the moment, mimicking a high realization that they do not have. It happens frequently around actual
crazy-wisdom lamas that students mistakenly think they have an
equal level of accomplishment. This huge mistake is no excuse
for crude behavior. Some of my teachers were undeniably fully
enlightened buddhas, but they never gave up the carefulness of
proper gentle behavior in accordance with the highest standards
of conduct. View and conduct need to be integrated. We need to
endeavor in positive deeds continuously and pay close attention

to what should be accepted and rejected in regards to cause and effect, harm and benefit.

Most importantly, we always need to keep in mind the futility of samsaric pursuits and the instability of ordinary happiness. We should never forget or ignore the fact that change, impermanence, and death are the only certainties for unrealized beings like us. We should not lose sight of the true focus, which is the exalted path to enlightenment for the benefit of all those unfortunates caught in samsaric existence. The more we dedicate ourselves to practice, the stronger our trust in the preciousness of the Dharma and the infallibility of these sublime teachings becomes. Devotion to our teachers and their instructions, and compassion for beings lost in the grip of delusion, should increase and develop deeply and unwaveringly as signs of progress.

To change our rigid minds takes continual mindfulness and dedication; otherwise, we easily fall back into the negative tendencies to which we have become habituated. Unfolding moment-by-moment, this process seems endless due to the thickness of our obscurations, but we should not be discouraged and we should never abandon the process, because then there wouldn't be any growth or improvement. As Trungpa Rinpoche has stated, "There is something funny about people saying that their lives have been completely changed: for instance the first time they had some experience, their lives have been completely transformed and changed. They bring up the idea that they want to discontinue what they are. They don't like what they were but they like what they are now. Experience is simply gone through. The Bardo experiences are not transformations of your life, they are continuity, and that continuity takes the shape of both highlights and the ordinary situations as well."[69]

Do not expect any instantaneous transformations or to be carried away by awesome experiences. Eventually, such phenomena prove to be temporary. They will vanish, leaving negative emotions still intact. Temporary experiences cannot purify delusion from the core. Only the practice of gathering the accumulations combined with devotion and compassion, embraced by wisdom, can give the ultimate result. Although the natural state need not be sought outside of us, we still need to be introduced to it, recognize it, and train in the proper recognition until we reach certainty. Stability in the unexcelled state of awareness is not attained independent of means and knowledge. The means is proper conduct; the knowledge is the proper view, which is only accomplished when view and conduct are united.

We need to respect relative truth in an intelligent way and examine how we stray into spiritual arrogance. As Dilgo Khyentse Rinpoche said, "When your realization of emptiness becomes as vast as the sky, you will gain an even greater conviction about the law of cause and effect, and you will see just how important your conduct really is. Relative truth functions inexorably within absolute truth. A thorough realization of the empty nature of all phenomena has never led anyone to think that positive actions do not bring happiness, or that negative actions do not bring suffering."[70]

Integration

I confess to not equalizing life and practice.

SOMEHOW, YOU AND I ended up in the Age of Strife, a time when people are not kind and friendly to one another, but fight amongst themselves and live under the rampant surge of the five degenerations.[71] To verify this, simply open a newspaper or turn on the news. Conflict, natural disaster, famine, sickness, and depravation intensify the general lack of altruism and merit. These have been consistent themes over the last hundred years. Our planet Earth is likewise suffering from pollution that has triggered global warming, threatening to end human existence as we have known it. Amidst all of this anxiety, it is not surprising that profound spiritual attainment is scarce. From my own side, I experience deep apprehensiveness from something as minor as losing electricity or water for a day or so while in retreat. Additionally, I never seem to drop the well-stocked pantry of negative thoughts and ego clinging. Rabid with useless mental gossip, how can I expect meaningful growth?

To summarize what you have read about me through the pages of this book: I was a child of the sixties who desperately tried to alter my fractured world. I felt social change was necessary in an American society that encouraged gross exploitation of peoples and resources worldwide as an extension of crass materialism and self-serving aggression. I maneuvered my way to the University of California at Berkeley at a time of political unrest and change, and I flirted with joining the radicals. After a demonstration I participated in ended in violence and death,

I decided that revolution was within. I needed to make radical internal changes in order to affect the external world.

Since childhood, I felt a deep wish to be of benefit to others. Having become a Buddhist, I steered away from New-Age spiritual fads. My friends at a commune gravitated toward an Indian guru who advocated a meditation technique whereby you experienced the "nectar." This nectar, as it was explained, would sustain you during the forthcoming apocalypse when others were starving. Yet, I was not motivated to save myself while others were dying.

Given my earlier vow and proclivity, I chose instead the more traditional path of Zen Buddhism. I liked the minimalism of Zen and only became a Tibetan Buddhist after years practicing Zen. In the beginning, I thought Tibetan Vajrayana Buddhism was too complicated, though I later found the same Zen simplicity embodied in many of the tantric masters I have been fortunate enough to meet.

So many years later, when examining myself, I see some progress, but not the great transformation I had envisioned when I began this journey. These days I have decided to backtrack a bit, and reintroduce many of the Mahayana methods that I took lightly. I will employ them as Dzigar Kongtrul Rinpoche instructs:

> The ideal way to practice is to put *lojong* [mind training] and Dzogchen practice hand in hand. Lojong is a relative practice working with thoughts and emotions, manipulating them in a positive direction. Do a lot of lojong practice during post-meditation, since one is more frequently in this state. As the stability of one's meditation practice increases, let go of the lojong practice and just have the meditation practice take care of your mind. I think that would be very good.

It seems that we still find old habitual reactions, even though we meditate a lot. That's why I think even though one practices Dzogchen, always having some mind training practice to assist the Dzogchen is very important. Otherwise some of that danger of reacting in old ways still seems to surface.[72]

Often I find myself training in a superficial way. Frequently, I have sat in the shrine room and breathed in the negative karmas and actions of all of sentient beings, altruistically exhaled all my happiness and well wishes, and then got up from the session and become annoyed by the first person I encountered! I have to remind myself of the need to put into action what I mentally create during meditation practice.

I have been frequently accused of being overconfident. My self-assurance bothers some people. The positive side of confidence, however, is that, when discouraged by my lack of development, I have only one place to revert to: back to the cushion and the attempt to generate a mindfulness that will translate into everyday life. Giving up is not an option. Neither is leaving the mindfulness on the practice cushion. As Tulku Urgyen Rinpoche notes,

> What happens is the changes that need to take place in our stream of being are neglected due to superficial application. It is not enough to call oneself a practitioner and let the time fly by. That is not the meaning of practicing the Dharma. We have been in samsara for countless lifetimes. Our minds have been so absorbed in the tendencies for samsaric existence, so, how can we expect to be totally transformed within a few years' time?

It does not happen like that. The habitual patterns, the three poisons and the dualistic fixations are all latent in our minds. They have been there, in continuous recreation, from time without beginning. Whenever a situation presents itself we are caught up again, and this occurs repeatedly, over and over.

Right now, our buddha nature is hidden. The only way to make buddha nature fully manifest is to continue practicing the Dharma in an authentic way. And this does not happen by only practicing off and on for a few years. Of course, sporadic practice does make nice imprints, but it does not generate authentic change to the depths of one's being.

To be discouraged because nothing extraordinary has happened since you began practicing is missing the point. Renunciation is the true sign of accomplishment, blessing and realization. In other words, there is a natural disenchantment with samsaric attainments, with any samsaric state.

Do not attach any importance to temporary experiences, not at all. There is only one thing to be confident in: the true state of realization that is unchanging like space. Understanding this is of utmost importance. What really matters is to increase your devotion to and confidence in the Dharma, so that from within you feel that only the Dharma matters, that only practice is important. That is a sure sign of accomplishment.

Always nurture the feeling, "For the rest of my life I will never give up the practice of the Dharma!" Forsaking Dharma practice can happen when an individual does not feel he or she can get anything out of it *for me, for myself.* Never give up the Dharma! When you travel to Bodhgaya by foot from Kathmandu, there are many ups and downs; it is not always easy. There are mountains, there are valleys, and there are rivers we have to cross. If you stop on the way, you will not get there. Traveling to Bodhgaya without getting sidetracked means to apply the view, meditation and conduct as often as possible. Continue your Dharma practice at a constant pace.

Please endeavor again and again to bring spiritual practice into every moment of your life. We often make this prayer, "May I equalize life and practice." Don't practice a little bit just once in a while, living the life of an ordinary person most of the time. Equalize life and practice! Fill every moment of your life with spiritual practice. In whatever you do, try again and again to let be in uncontrived naturalness. If you stop somewhere along the way, you might end up in dusty Raxoul at the Nepali border, and never reach Bodhgaya itself. Train in recognizing your buddha nature, and you will one day arrive at the Bodhgaya of true and complete enlightenment.[73]

As a reminder to myself to help bring spiritual practice into *every moment* of life, I will attempt to restate some advice I have received from my teachers. Please understand that we live in a period of "mere resemblance," when contact with any likeness of the Dharma is meritorious and, regrettably, all we have to work with. We were not fortunate enough to be liberated at the time of the Buddha or Padmasambhava, so like it or not, we have no other choice.

As it has been said, to be a genuine practitioner necessitates giving up attachment to this life and to the consideration that relative phenomena are meaningful. Unfortunately, in my case, I still do not consistently believe in the pointlessness of samsara. I hold on to the belief that the next thing will make me happy, secure, and fulfilled and that I will find something in conditioned existence that is consequential and totally significant. Until now, I have been unable to abandon this strong fixation and hope; hence, I cannot abandon samsara. Dzongsar Khyentse Rinpoche addresses just this point: "We are continuously beaten back by circumstances and struggles. We have to recognize samsara as dangerous. If we accept samsara as a hideous cliff that we are falling off of, we will change our value system. But not many people really want enlightenment; they merely want to have a better life."[74]

With these words in mind, I will attempt to describe in a practical way what it means to mingle Dharma and daily activities, or equalize life and practice. From the perspective of the Great Perfection, Dzogchen, no division exists between meditation sessions and breaks. One maintains awareness in an unbroken continuity throughout all times and all situations. For most of us who are unstable in our recognition of *rigpa*[75], or not even sure of having experienced it, that is a burning aspiration rather than a realistic actuality.

There are several helpful ways to integrate our recognition of awareness and our contemplative meditation practice into our daily existence. The most convenient system is to divide the day into four periods that correspond to the natural progression of light. This is compatible with an instruction titled *Four Sessions that Equalize Buddhahood,* referring to dawn, daytime, dusk, and nighttime. "Equalizing Buddhahood" means that if you can practice these four, then you are never apart from the buddhas:

"At dawn, revive the natural awareness," means waking up from the sleep of ignorance by imagining the sound of music played by the *daḳas* and dakinis jingling their *damarus* and bells. Thereafter try to visualize your teacher in the sky before you and, after supplicating, receive the four empowerments from the four places of his or her body and remain in awareness as much as possible. This is a method to invigorate your mind and sharpen your basic intelligence.

Next, "sealing experiences during daytime," means to loosen our anxiety-ridden approach to daily occurrences by viewing them without hope and fear in an awake, mindful way. Another method of practicing with everyday life, according to a Mahayana approach, is to acknowledge everything as an illusion: an illusory person doing illusory activities. This helps to deconstruct our strong habitual tendency of solidifying all experience as real.

To "spontaneously withdraw the senses at dusk" has to do, in this context, with inner heat practice or *tummo.* But those of us unfamiliar with *tummo* practice can, at dusk, remember impermanence. Think how nothing lasts and all things change. Then bring renunciation to mind, contemplating the futility of all unreal samsaric pursuits. Let go of all aims and goals and remain in a gentle openness free of all objectives.

Finally, "at nighttime retain wakefulness in the vase." This means going to sleep while imagining a luminous white syllable AH in your heart center. As its light radiates, try to fall asleep in awareness.[76] By applying these four sessions throughout the day and night, we will never be separate from the buddhas.

Cutting ego clinging and deep-rooted ignorance from its source is a penetrating and thorough undertaking. It can be slow and painful, and is not achieved quickly or by superficial methods. Do not get disheartened if you do not experience results immediately. Its profundity makes the task a long and drawn out one, but ultimately this is what will make it most effective. We shouldn't be too hard on ourselves—we are not producing superficial, cosmetic improvements; rather, we are destroying the source of samsara, and that takes powerful, persistent measures to annihilate all the ingrown habits. Continue diligently and pray for the discipline to overcome laziness and doubts. Especially when we have difficulties with other people and cannot see a way out of the turmoil, we must remain in impartiality and make aspirations to benefit them. In this way, accumulate merit and dedicate it on their behalf.

On occasion, when I fall into the dark-night-of-the-soul syndrome (i.e., discouragement), and question my practice and attainments, I remember something Tulku Urgyen Rinpoche explained. He called this the practitioner who has been hit by a "frost" of the spirit; it is quite common, and it needs to be intentionally overcome. During these times, we need to identify beyond a doubt that this frame of mind is an obstacle. Deliberately apply the methods to move away from this mental gloom. Pray to Padmasambhava or your root teacher, supplicating wholeheartedly and taking the four empowerments, repeatedly if necessary. Like with all temporary experiences, being aware and not grasping too tightly will cause this "frost" to pass. Adeu Rinpoche advises,

> As one is not truly advanced, there is fluctuation.
> This is just a sign of not having reached a state
> of stability. There are ups and downs; sometimes

one feels successful in applying the instructions, and other times one feels completely ineffectively engaged in the training. This is how it is, sometimes one is more capable than other times, feeling that practice went well, other times feeling that it did not.

Milarepa told Rechungpa, "Your meditation is like a vulture soaring: occasionally it is high and other times it nears the ground." So if even Rechungpa had variability in his meditative state, there is no question about us. Don't worry about this, simply carry on and apply the teachings.

However, it is possible to make things even more problematic by being delighted when there is an alleged success and depressed when there is an apparent failure. This indulging in accepting and rejecting will make it even worse. Being attached to remembering the instructions and then punishing yourself for not performing perfectly is completely unnecessary. This is an extraneous, self-inflicted trouble; do not add to the difficulty in this way. Simply carry on, thinking that when we are able to remember the instructions, it is thanks to the guru's oral instructions. When we do not remember, make a prayer that you will remember better next time.[77]

Always consider that practicing the Dharma is like a precious treasure, a set of positive circumstances and conditions that come together to nurture us. It is a joyous affirmation of our potential that stirs from the depths of our being to guide us. To act upon that steadfastness is the confluence of countless lifetimes of aspirations and good wishes. That we even have the merit to encounter the teachers and the teachings is the result of incredibly excellent karma from previous lives.

I often think how difficult it is to give up the instant gratification and comfortable lifestyle in which I am ensconced, and to separate myself from the seemingly pleasurable things that dissipate my time. I readily indulge in swift communication, e-mail, Internet, exciting media, music, movies, and friends. To take steps away from all of this god-realm activity, I need to galvanize an amazing amount of discipline and conviction. There always seems to be one more extremely important project to take care of—and of course, finances to consider.

Because it is quite difficult to attain stability in practice while distracted by everyday life, occasionally do serious practice in retreat to enhance this regular effort. Seek a solitary place with minimal disturbances or a Dharma community with like-minded Dharma friends. In the past in India and Tibet, great yogis and teachers went to different places to practice virtuous disciplines. They often attained realization and accomplishment, thus blessing these places. Today, pilgrims journey to these holy places to receive their blessings and enhance their own practice.[78] In such places, practice is improved by an intensification of mindfulness, and positive results are created from the auspicious links and blessings. Sacred places are extremely significant for the affirmative influence of their environments that stem from the very subtle interdependence of everything.[79] A place committed to the pursuit of positive, revered ideals where people engage in worship, respect, and veneration emanates benefit to its immediate surroundings as it also generates intangible hallowed energy.

Retreat promotes simplicity and helps the practitioner transition from proactive worldly busyness to the contemplative lifestyle of a meditator. One's whole focus and emphasis transforms along with the physical body, the breath, and the mental patterns. Instead of directing the attention outwardly, one reverses this continual projection towards the refinement of inner development. The change is dramatic. A practitioner's corporal language and way of operating is drastically different from those of mundane people, especially the awake glimmer in his or her eyes. Slowing down and cutting activities to a minimum brings us much closer to our own mind, and as external distractions cease, we merely need to contend with the internal, albeit formidable, dialogue. Diminished diversions and preoccupations allow true spiritual development, which is why there is so much emphasis on going to quiet places of solitude to do serious training.

However, to reach stability and full maturity, practice has to be mingled totally with daily life, which is the outcome of dedicated training. Often the famous statement of Kagyü meditators is repeated: "When I am in the mountains in retreat, my meditation is nondistracted and vast, but when I am in the city, my meditation is left in the mountains!"

Of course, the choice to practice in a retreat situation can be problematic, even unpleasant at times. There is the inconvenience of things breaking; crises with water or energy; noisy, annoying neighbors; lack of proper supplies and support. When encountering such things, I carry on. After the first few days of tumult, I settle in and marvel at the wonder of having persevered, and then I concentrate on practice. I can confirm that not every day is great. There are ups and downs, elations and melancholy, but I simply continue. Lerab Lingpa states some essential points about retreat: "No matter how isolated the environment is, if you continually waste your time by carelessly involving your body, speech, and mind in superficial distractions and laziness, or by secretly indulging in negative thoughts and behavior, you are dishonest with yourself, which is an enormous shortcoming. So that applying yourself to practice will prove meaningful, make a firm vow in retreat, removed from ordinary and superficial thought and behavior, to be always stable in being mindful, alert, and careful."[80]

Even though you might think that you have a time limit or a set number to amass, don't focus on the result. One finishes when all obscurations are purified and accumulations gathered, stability is reached, and enlightenment and the ability to act effortlessly for the benefit of beings have been attained. So for me at least, the journey will continue for quite a while. Use the time in retreat to collect questions that a teacher can clarify. Always make the wish to equalize life and practice.

Never give up the aspiration to become fully enlightened in this lifetime. Avoid imitating what Khandro Rinpoche describes as the modern Tibetan way of practicing:

> If you are satisfied with what Tibetans have been able to come to terms with, if it is the same, then it is not a problem at all. As Tibetans, in these 1,200 years of Tibetan Buddhism, we have come to a point where many of us know we are probably going to die without getting enlightened. Therefore the best we can hope for is another precious human life near a teacher with good conditions, close to the Dharma; basically, we aspire for all the qualities we have now. Because we don't want to bring about real personal transformation, we begin to hope for another chance. Sometimes I tease the Tibetan monks and nuns that it has taken us 1,200 years to give up hope about enlightenment in one lifetime; instead we anticipate another chance.

When I grew up I was amazed at some of the Western students who would come, receive teachings, and diligently practice them. Westerners were not like Tibetans then. I remember being in rooms receiving teachings where each individual Westerner would absolutely be convinced that they could do it in one week. People would sit in front of the teacher, and whatever the teacher taught, they would practice. We would receive the same teachings together with the Westerners. We were very young, and so we didn't hope for much. We used to pack the texts and go and try to do a little bit of what was said, but we were never really serious about it. However, several of the Westerners would go out and do whatever the teacher told them to do.

I grew up marveling and often being very fascinated with how strong their enthusiasm was. Sometimes I asked them and they would reply, "Well, it says you can attain enlightenment in one lifetime, so the teachings must be right. If they say you can do it, you can do it." Today Westerners have all changed; I don't see that initial enthusiasm any more. We see more of the Western practitioners becoming like our generation of Tibetans. We hope for a better life next time. It has only taken Westerners forty or more years to transition to the same mind-set that took Tibetans 1,200 years to arrive at.[81]

Retreat at Samye Chimphu, Tibet, 1986

View from retreat hut at Nagi Nunnery, Nepal

Nagi Nunnery, winter

Nagi Nunnery, spring

Yes to Possibilities

*I confess to not being open to the present moment
and the potential therein.*

All of the realized masters that I have had the good fortune to encounter have exhibited certain undeniable characteristics in common—humility, regal dignity, sharpness of intellect, overflowing compassion and love, unwavering faith in the Three Jewels and the infallibility of karma, as well as incomparable appreciation for their teachers and the teachings. These qualities are not mind-blowing, astounding, miracle-producing spectacles, but are the core of what accomplishment is about. Being in the presence of such amazing individuals is like basking in the warmth of sunshine on a freezing day and is no different than being magnetized by the sparkling, heartrending sincerity displayed by enlightenment. They are representations of the physical embodiment of purity, effortless mindfulness, and carefulness. They exhibit diligence in fully intermingling life and practice, selflessly fulfilling the benefit of beings. As Thinley Norbu Rinpoche explains, "Even if we use ordinary intellectual power, when we meet with people who use pure noble intelligent power, we automatically get a sense of expansiveness rather than one of rejection or confinement to a lower level. In this way, some pure and gifted meditators create a field of bliss around themselves through their spontaneous luminous power, and use their pure elements to help others attain the same level and join with them in the same mandala and same mind."[82]

The energy, openness, and empathy of these masters are the results of having overcome ignorance and any speck of ego clinging, self-protection, and aggression. These qualities accommodate a fearlessness that can deal with all situations without being threatened or humiliated. An example of this is given by Dilgo Khyentse Rinpoche: "Many Buddhist teachers were abused, treated as criminals, and beaten when the Chinese communists came to Tibet. Instead of feeling hatred, they prayed that the negative actions of all beings would be purified through the vindictive attacks against them."[83]

Once ignorance has been purified and self-clinging vanquished, the possibilities are limitless like space. This vastness is the reality of a realized yogi. We, conversely, are limited like the space held firmly in the grip of our hands, as we clench our fists in desperation, trying to establish our worth and validity in unaware, erroneous terms. Let's review this road map that leads to the exalted state of a realized yogi where everything is possible and attainable.

Earlier in the book, ground was defined as the basis of all, the original purity. Enlightened beings have never strayed from this state of primordial purity, whereas sentient beings became separated from it by "not recognizing their own naturally occurring self-manifestation of the great empty original purity."[84] This marks the delineation between buddhas and beings: buddhas are undeluded, while beings have fallen under the power of confusion. To become re-enlightened, we must undergo the path of trainings that purify the obscurations we have collected as a result of nonrecognition. Yogis take hold of the path and endeavor to cleanse the temporary stains. Once these stains are purified and the accumulations perfected, realized yogis attain the result or the fruition by being reestablished in the innate pure nature.

Because we misconstrued pure phenomena, it solidified into gross commonly accepted phenomena and sentient beings split away from the natural state. Everything was divided up into subject and object. Dualistic mind increasingly fortifies its deluded habits and strays further and further away from the basic ground of awareness wisdom. So, our original body, speech, and mind that were no different from the enlightened body, speech, and mind of all the buddhas have become increasingly coarse and rough and are what we experience now as the body of flesh and blood, fragmented speech, and bewildered mind. We can return to our pure state because it is the source from which we strayed. In fact, all relative things originate from the ultimate.[85] If this were not the case, we could never become re-enlightened, just as it is impossible to turn sand into a diamond.

We can easily understand how our experience is different from that of the Buddha, but how do we differ from an accomplished yogi traversing the path? The various Dzogchen instruction manuals explain that thoughts occur in the same way for ordinary people and yogis; however, whereas ordinary people are carried away by thoughts, a yogi is trained in the key instruction of liberation of thought at the time of arising. The common analogy is that a yogi's thoughts are like drawings on water, disappearing the moment they are formed. For the rest of us, thoughts are like drawings in stone—they are carved deeply and imprinted. This is how we encounter reality. We live with our minds, so this is not foreign to us. Thoughts are being created morning until evening, and rerun endlessly with a strong tendency to be taken as true and concrete. We reinforce thoughts by a continual repetition of our point of view, over and over and over again. Even when we are not under the influence of coarse thoughts, we walk around with a subtle narrator who constantly refers back to ourselves and incessantly evaluates that which is seemingly beneficial or harmful to us.

Initiating intellectual investigation and effort to dismantle the solidity of self, thoughts, and perceptions helps to lighten this tight grip of grasping, as all spiritual practices do. But to totally destroy delusion from the root and to become reestablished in the exalted state of enlightenment in this very body and lifetime, *rigpa* needs to be introduced, recognized, and trained in until this innate self-originating awareness is stabilized. Realized yogis have done this, and that is the primary reason why they experience phenomena so differently than we do. As Tulku Urgyen Rinpoche has taught,

> The simple definition of mind is the unity of being emptiness and cognizance; it is complete within that sentence. Its essence is empty; its nature is cognizant; its capacity is that these two cannot be taken apart. That is the meaning of unity—impossible to separate; emptiness and cognizance cannot be divided. That is the state of affairs in all beings, yet they do not experience it.
>
> As is stated in the *Mahaprajnaparamita*, "Transcendental knowledge (*prajnaparamita*), which is inexpressible, inconceivable, and indescribable, nonarising and nonceasing, is the essence of space itself." It is the experience of individual cognizance, self-cognizant wakefulness or wisdom. In the case of sentient beings, it is the experience of an individual ignorance, but for yogis it is the unity of emptiness and cognizance suffused with awareness; for sentient beings it is emptiness and cognizance suffused with ignorance.[86]

As we know, our way of operating is through subject-object fixation and grasping, always reinforcing the ego's impressions. A yogi is aware of all that transpires, but does not obsess upon it, follow after objects of perception, or get carried away by discursive thinking. Yogis are not zombies: their senses are wide open and alert, but the incessant inner dialogue has ceased, and thought movement, which is freed upon arising, does not control them. Khenpo Tsultrim Gyatso explains a yogi's perception as follows:

> Mind is the mode of cognition that is involved with a distinctly apprehended subject, awareness the mode of cognition that transcends such a split. Mind is conceptual; awareness transcends conceptual cognition. From the ultimate point of view, mind is considered an obscuration, awareness a self-arisen wisdom that is aware of itself. For such wisdom, what is aware is in no way distinct from what it is aware of. It is cognition that has the capacity to directly and fully recognize and rest in its own nature.
>
> The awareness of the lack of self-nature is called yogic direct valid cognition; it is aware of the nature of things, the emptiness of the apprehended and the apprehending.[87]

Mingyur Rinpoche concludes through science as well as meditation that:

> Clinical studies indicate that the practice of meditation extends the mechanism of neuronal synchrony to a point where the perceiver can begin to recognize consciously that his or her mind and the experiences or objects that his or her mind perceives are one and the same. In other words,

the practice of meditation over a long period dissolves artificial distinctions between subject and object—which in turn offers the perceiver the freedom to determine the quality of his or her own experience, the freedom to distinguish between what is real and what is merely an appearance.

Dissolving the distinction between subject and object, however, doesn't mean that perception becomes a great big blur. You still continue to perceive experience in terms of subject and object, while at the same time recognizing that the distinction is essentially conceptual. In other words, the perception of an object is not different from the mind that perceives it. . . .

In the same way, in waking life, transcending the distinction between subject and object is equivalent to recognizing that whatever you experience is not separate from the mind that experiences it. Waking life doesn't stop, but your experience or perception of it shifts from one of limitation to one of wonder and amazement.[88]

How do we arrive at the same level that realized yogis who have taken hold of the undeluded wisdom aspect of their minds achieve, and maintain that in all situations of meditation practice and daily life? We practitioners on the path need to do the same, and reconnect with our essential nature and train in it. We need to make sincere supplications to our teachers to have the merit to receive the blessings to meet buddha nature and then apply that correct recognition diligently in practice so that "dualistic habit is reduced and nondualistic wisdom phenomena expands."[89] The more we train in sustaining the continuity of wisdom awareness, the less our grasping and fixating mind will control us, and we draw closer to a yogi's pure experience, which is open and free. As Tulku Urgyen Rinpoche describes, for a yogi, *rigpa* becomes easy to recognize and maintain. "Yogi means having some degree of stability in the recognition of *rigpa*. For such a practitioner, everything looks different. Reality is different from how ordinary people believe it to be and experience it. Padmasambhava and Milarepa were not obstructed by what we believe to be solid matter. The seeming solidity of their own bodies and the seeming solidity of matter were totally interpenetrable. They could walk on water and were unharmed by fire."[90]

Those of us who have committed to this path have the incredibly great fortune to have encountered the precious teachings of the Buddha as well as living teachers who offer us the opportunity to study those teachings and assist us in training in them. Such a situation is a source of rejoicing that fills my heart with gratitude. It doesn't matter that the path is long and difficult; it is the journey itself that is important. We must keep mindfulness as a constant guide and stay determined not to give up until reaching the exalted state. What a destination it is: to arrive at the state of a realized yogi and eventually Buddhahood, where there are no opponents, no strivings, where we can act for the benefit of others without premeditation, since we have nothing to hold on to, cherish, or protect. We have put so much effort into propping up the unreal and reinforcing such a pointless pursuit. How sad and ironic—now we can rise above that.

These days, we also have the fortunate situation of technology that works to our advantage for the study of the Dharma. There are incredible supports in media, audio and video files, Web sites bursting with information, and of course books and transcripts. Many dedicated translators have produced practice materials, commentaries, and *sadhanas* for us in our native languages. It is impressive and inspiring. All these opportunities to learn, review, and contemplate are essential. Thanks to podcasts and webcasts, we are never far from our teachers and their teachings, though they are on the other side of the world.

However, there is no substitute for direct contact and an ongoing relationship with a living teacher. So it is critical to find the right teacher and create the time to ask questions to clarify any doubts. Any opportunity should be seized with him or her to discuss practice and any obstacles that may have arisen. One should not waste time with the teacher talking about mundane situations, such as office or domestic problems, especially if one has had the great merit to be introduced to the nature of mind and actually recognize it. One should not leave it with that one time, but continually train, as much as possible, in meditation sessions and daily-life experiences. As Lerab Lingpa advises, "Rely on authentic holy lamas who are learned and accomplished and whose motivation is altruistic. For the rest of your life, do not waver from seeking out such masters and hearing teachings directly from them."[91]

To paraphrase an insightful statement by Suzuki Roshi, "In the beginner's mind there are many possibilities, in the expert's mind very few." Every moment that we are alive is a fresh opportunity for renewal, change, and rebirth. We continually have the chance to break away from standardized patterns, but we don't seize the opening. Instead we fall into the comfort of habit that undermines the possibility of our liberation. Such dualistic patterns ruin us, moment after moment, day after day, life after life, shackling us to samsara's prison, from which we could break out if we simply demolished the chains of grasping to solidity and awakened to our innate nature. Tulku Urguyen Rinpoche says, "To be a true yogi is to connect with that which is naturally so, bringing the natural state into actual experience. Once you have recognized the natural state—in other words, once it is an actuality in your living experience—people can truly say, 'The yogi has arrived,' when you walk into a room! Your body is still that of a human being, but your mind is free."[92]

Tulku Thondup Rinpoche tells the story of a great yogi named Chatralwa (literally, "the renunciate") who was visited one day by a lama who could not reconcile the hermit's comfortable life with his name. Sensing the lama's discomfort, the yogi asked him what the matter was. The lama responded, "I heard that you are a hermit, but in fact, you have collected enough to be called a rich man." Chatralwa replied, "A renunciate [*chatralwa*] is someone who has gotten rid of his or her emotional attachments to worldly goods or to life itself. It does not mean being poor and hankering for them as many do."[93]

We strayed progressively from the primordial state to arrive at where we are at present, but we have the opportunity to regain control of our destinies, reverse this downward spiral, and return to our true nature. All the practices, aspirations, and teachings are conduits for the key point of the view, which once recognized and trained in, we can actualize in practice and daily life. Eventually as stability in the natural state is established, everything becomes the expression of *rigpa*. Bring to mind the teaching that Tilopa gave to Naropa: "Experiences do not harm you, clinging to them does. So cut your clinging, Naropa." Once we have established the natural state, then we can say yes to possibilities, because all experience is a sublime cause for the accumulation of merit. When ignorance is purified, ego fixation has ceased, and subject and object are gone, all phenomena are experienced as the pure display of awareness wisdom.

Acknowledgments

I HAVE INADEQUATELY REPEATED in this book teachings that I have heard, learned, studied, and practiced under great masters. I have not presented anything new, unique, or original that I made up or am unfamiliar with, if there are mistakes and undue repetition, I apologize for these errors; I express regret for my vast limitations. Beyond a doubt, I acknowledge that sublime teachers have said it all before, more wisely, movingly, and with much more stable conviction, I merely parrot their brilliance in my feeble way. Having been truly inspired by the authenticity and relevance of the Buddhist teachings and trainings, I deeply believe that assuming even one of them will inwardly change people and outwardly change the world.

I was joined in this effort by several wonderful friends and teachers to whom I owe thanks: first of all to Tulku Thondup, who wrote the brilliant foreword and offered many insightful suggestions; to Pepe Trevor, the gifted writer who inspired me with her careful recommendations; to James Hopkins for improving the wording and catching inconsistencies; to Susan Griffin, another wonderful writer, who tried to teach me the art of writing; to Meghan Howard, the eagle eyed copy editor who amazes me with her sharpness; to David Leskovitz for polishing the language; to Joan Olson, my book designer and reliable typesetter; to the consistent proof readers, Alex Yiannopoulos, Meryl Dowman and Gloria Jones; to Maryann Lipaj, whose artistic eye creates beautiful covers.

Not possessing any qualities, either of learning or realization through practice and study, I nevertheless enjoy a profound delight and appreciation for the words of the Buddha and great masters. Hoping to share some of that enthusiasm and likewise infect others, I undertook to compose this book. I have tried to rephrase theories and instructions minimally while still maintaining some modicum of their beauty, expressiveness, and purity. With sincere devotion and love, I offer whatever I may have gleaned as droplets of water in a time of drought, walking the path as the dreg that I am at the end of this Dark Age. I only pray that there may be some benefit for beings and that we all can meet at the glorious Copper Colored Mountain in the presence of the Lotus Master without losing the way.

Completed on the thirteenth anniversary of the passing into nirvana of our precious teacher, Kyabje Tulku Urgyen Rinpoche, may his reincarnation blaze with the splendor of his predecessor!

APPENDICES

Appendix 1

Vipashyana

As you may have undoubtedly noticed throughout this book, I have a great love and esteem for the Dzogchen teachings. I have not the slightest doubt that if practiced correctly, Dzogchen is one of the swiftest and most supreme paths to enlightenment. However, though I have studied these teachings and have a sound intellectual understanding of them, I do not in any way feel qualified to give any sort of pithy instruction other than duplicating and quoting realized masters and texts affiliated with this tradition.

Because I left out vipashyana training, except for the mere mention of it, I would like to try to clarify some of the most common misunderstandings associated with its practice. Tulku Urgyen Rinpoche teaches, "each vehicle, beginning with the Hinayana upwards, has its own particular view, meditation, and conduct. Each has the same aim, to understand emptiness; and each employs practices called *shamatha* and *vipashyana*."[94] Although I have barely studied *vipassana*, the variant spelling of which denotes the vipashyana traditions of the lesser vehicles, that is taught in the insight meditation centers in the West, I have nevertheless come to understand that a subtle concept is always held in mind in that practice. Whether it is labeled mindfulness or remaining aware of the present moment, this conceptuality is the main difference between this type of vipassana and the Tibetan vipashyana.

Tulku Urgyen Rinpoche goes on to elucidate further the differences between shamatha and vipashyana as practiced in the lower schools and as practiced in Dzogchen:

> On the Mahayana level, the ultimate shamatha and vipashyana is called the "shamatha and vipashyana that delights the Tathagatas." Though the same names are used, their depth is much superior to the shamatha and vipashyana employed in the shravaka system. Every vehicle practices shamatha and vipashyana, so don't think that at the level of Dzogchen these two are ignored or left out. On the contrary, on the Ati level, the innate stability in *rigpa,* the nondual state of awareness, is the shamatha aspect, while the awake or cognizant quality is the vipashyana aspect.

> The principle we must understand here is stated like this: "Same word, superior meaning." Shamatha and vipashyana are ultimately indivisible. Both are naturally included and practiced in Ati Yoga. The extraordinary shamatha here is to resolve and rest in the true emptiness itself. We do not merely get the idea of emptiness; in actuality, in direct experience, we resolve emptiness and rest naturally in that state. Naturally resting is the genuine shamatha of not creating anything artificial whatsoever, of simply remaining in the experience of emptiness. And vipashyana means not to deviate or depart from that state.

> The difference in the levels of practice depends on the degree to which conceptual mind is in-

volved. The differences between the vehicles are not marked by using the same terminology but by the use of progressively superior levels of meaning. That is why the Buddha said about the nine vehicles, "My teachings are a gradual progression from the beginning up to the highest perfection, like the steps on a staircase that extend from the lowest to the highest, or like a newborn infant who slowly grows up."[95]

In the investigative techniques of vipashyana in the Mahamudra system, the student first works with mind mixed with awareness and is eventually led to separate these two, at which occasion the teacher can then give the pointing-out instruction. According to Thrangu Rinpoche, in the vipashyana of the Mahamudra system,

> the investigation of the calm and the moving mind is a method used to introduce and recognize the nature of mind. . . .
>
> This endeavor of investigation should yield some attainment. At best, one attains realization about the nature of mind. The middling type of person gains some experience of how the nature of mind is. One should at least, as a person of lesser capacity, reach a stable understanding, be convinced about the nature of mind. Though being intellectually convinced does not, in itself, lead to realization, it may help to encourage one to pursue the training until realizing the true meditation state. But it is not enough merely to understand; direct experience is required to actualize the real

meditation state within oneself. Why? Because it is the meditation state that purifies shortcomings and obscurations, through which one progresses along the path of enlightenment.[96]

With Dzogchen, one is introduced to awareness from the very beginning—pure, unadulterated *rigpa*—and if the recognition of the natural state is correct, that is what one unerringly trains in. Tulku Urgyen Rinpoche explains,

> According to ordinary shamatha and vipashyana, shamatha is first cultivated and then vipashyana is pursued. Cultivating shamatha means to produce a state of mental stillness, and then to train in it. Pursuing or seeking the insight of vipashyana means to try to find who the meditator is; trying to identify what it is that remains quiet. It's evident that both of these practices are pretty much involved in conceptual thinking. Only in the Essence Mahamudra and Dzogchen systems is emptiness left without fabrication. In Dzogchen, from the very first, emptiness is resolved without any need to manufacture it. It emphasizes stripping awareness to its naked state, and not clinging to emptiness in any way whatsoever. The true and authentic vipashyana is the empty and cognizant nature of mind.[97]

Noble Tara statue

Appendix 2

Tara Liturgies

THE MANDALA RITUAL from the mind treasure of the profound essence of Tara,[98] extracted from the *Essence of the Two Accumulations*

Liturgy Instructions on what to do are noted in italics.

Repeat refuge three times:

NAMO

In the Noble Lady, embodiment of all Precious Ones,
I and all beings take refuge.
I form the resolve aspiring to enlightenment,
And I will enter the profound path.

Then say the mandala offering:

OM AH HUNG
Three realms and worlds, the beings and their splendor,
My body, wealth, and all my goodness,
I give to you who have compassion;
Accept them and bestow your blessings.
OM SARVA TATHAGATA RATNA MANDALA PUJA HOH

With that, present the specific mandala offering, and then chant the "Homage in Twenty-one Verses" from the Tantra of the King of Praise.

Having presented the mandala as above, then say:

Her right hand, in the *mudra* of supreme giving,
Turns into the gesture of giving refuge,
Which covers me and all those to be protected,
Assuring us of relief from all threats.

While imagining this, chant the "Homage in Twenty-one Verses."

Having again presented the mandala as above, then say:

A stream of nectar flows from her body,
Enters me and those to be protected through the crown
    of the head and completely fills our bodies,
So that we receive all of her blessings without exception.

While imagining this, chant the "Homage in Twenty-one Verses."

At the end:

The front visualization melts into light and dissolves
    into me.
With the blessings to be indivisible,
I turn into the form of Noble Tara,
Visible and yet insubstantial.

While you keep in mind the vivid presence and pride of being the Noble Lady yourself, recite the mantra in ten syllables as many times as you can.

OM TARE TUTTARE TURE SOHA

With that, make the dedication and aspiration.

Through this virtue may I quickly
Accomplish the state of Noble Tara.
Each and every being, with no exception,
May I bring to that same state.

Like the wish-fulfilling jewel and the vase of bounty,
Unimpeded, every wish you do fulfill.
Noble Tara, Conquerors, and offspring,
Bestow the auspiciousness of being forever nurtured
   by your compassion.

Homage in Twenty-one Verses

OM
Noble and exalted Tara,
I bow to you.

Homage to Tara, swift and courageous!
Who dispels all fears by the syllables TUTTARA,
The savioress who bestows all benefit by TURE,
With the syllables of homage, SOHA, I bow to you.

Homage to Tara, swift and courageous,
Whose gaze is as quick as a flash of lightning,
Who, on a tear from the face of the Protector of the
    Three Worlds,[99]
Arose from a billionfold lotus pistil.

Homage to her whose face is like a gathering
Of one hundred autumn full moons,
Who, like a cluster of one thousand stars,
Blazes light illuminating everything.

Homage to her, adorned by a lotus hand,[100]
Holding a golden blue lotus.
She is the scope of giving, perseverance,
Fortitude, patience, and meditation.

Homage to her, who moves in endless victory
As the crown of the Tathagatas.
Having obtained all transcendent virtues,
The sons of the jinas resort to her.

Homage to her who by the TUTTARA and HUNG syllables

Fills all space, directions, and desire realms.
While trampling the seven worlds under her feet,
She brings all and everything under her control.

Homage to her whom Indra, Agni, Brahma,
Marut, and Vishveshvara worship.
Ghosts, zombies, gandharvas, gana and yakshas
Pay tribute before her.

Homage to her who by TRAT and PHAT
Vanquishes evil forces conjured by magic.
Right leg bent, extended left leg trampling,
She destroys them completely with her intense blazing
    fire.

Homage to the swift, greatly fearsome one,
Who vanquishes the most tenacious of maras.
When she knits her brows on her lotus face,
She defeats all enemies.

Homage to her whose fingers adorn her heart,
In the mudra of the Three Jewels.
Her own light-beams fill her,
Ornamenting all directional wheels.

Homage to her, who disperses boundless joy
From the sparkling garland of lights on her crown.
From the great clangor of laughter with the TUTTARA
    syllables,
She brings demons and the world under her control.

Homage to her who can draw near
The gathering of all earth's protectors.

By the wrathful quake of the HUNG in her frown,[101]
She liberates all destitute beings.

Homage to her whose crescent-moon tiara
And all ornaments sparkle brilliantly,
Who from Amitabha atop her vast stream of hair,
Floods forth immense rays of light.

Homage to her, engulfed in a fire like the kalpa's end,
Who sits in the midst of a wreath of flames.
With right outstretched and left leg bent, she totally
    defeats
The numerous enemies of all who rejoice when the
    Dharma Wheel turns.

Homage to her, who strikes the earth with the palms,
And crushes it under her feet,
Who by HUNG and her wrathful glare,
Rules the beings of the sevenfold world-system.

Homage to her, the blissful, virtuous, and peaceful
    mother,
Whose activity is nirvana's sphere of tranquility.
By the flawless expression of SOHA and OM,
She overcomes even the greatest evil.

Homage to her who smashes
The bodies of the enemies that imprison joy,[102]
Illuminated[103] by the awareness HUNG
Arranged within a mantra of ten syllables.

Homage to the swift one: When she stamps her foot,
Her seed in the form of the syllable HUNG

Shakes the three worlds
And the Meru, Mandara, and Vindya mounts.

Homage to her in whose hands is placed the one who
    bears a deer mark[104]
In the shape of a godly lake.
She annuls every poison
With the twice-uttered TARA and the sound PHAT.[105]

Homage to her, served by the ruler of the host of deities,
By gods and kinnaras.[106]
The dazzling brightness, her armor of joy,
Dispels all quarrels and nightmares.

Homage to her like the full sun and moon,
Whose two eyes shine with blazing light.
By TUTTARA together with HARA recited twice,
She eliminates even the vilest sickness.

Homage to her, endowed with the power to perfectly
    pacify
Through the arrangement of the three thatnesses.
The crowds of demons, zombies, and yakshas
Are suppressed by TURE, the supreme mother.

These are the praises with the root mantra and the
    twenty-one verses of homage.

The "Homage in Twenty-one Verses" was translated from the Tibetan by Marcia Dechen Wangmo based on many existing translations and with the generous help of the Sanskrit pandit Mattia Salvini, the up saka Jñ nagarbha, and advice from the Maha Lotsawa, Erik Pema Kunsang. May it benefit countless beings!

Works Cited

Allen, Charles. *The Buddha and the Sahibs: The Men Who Discovered India's Lost Religion*. London: John Murray Publishers, 2002.

Binder Schmidt, Marcia, ed. and comp. *Dzogchen Essentials*. Hong Kong: Rangjung Yeshe Publications, 2004.

————, ed. and comp. *Dzogchen Primer*. Boston: Shambhala Publications, 2002.

Boorstein, Sylvia. "Tamara's Joy." *Shambhala Sun,* May 2008, 25.

Chogyam Trungpa. *The Collected Works of Chogyam Trungpa*. 8 vols. Boston: Shambhala Publications, 2003.

————. *The Sanity We Are Born With*. Compiled and edited by Carolyn Gimian. Boston: Shambhala Publications, 2005.

————. *Transcending Madness*. Boston: Shambhala Publications, 1992.

Chokgyur Lingpa. *Ocean of Amrita: Ngakso Puja*. Translated by Erik Pema Kunsang. Katmandu: Rangjung Yeshe Translations, 1998.

Dakpo Tashi Namgyal. *Clarifying the Natural State*. Translated by Erik Pema Kunsang. Hong Kong: Rangjung Yeshe Publications, 2002.

Dilgo Khyentse Rinpoche. *The Mind Ornament of Samantabhadra*. Translated by Erik Pema Kunsang. Katmandu: Rangjung Yeshe Publications, 1995.

————. *Heart Treasure of Compassion*. Translated by the Padmakara Translation Group. Boston: Shambhala Publications, 2007.

————. *Zurchungpa's Testament*. Translated by the Padmakara Translation Group. Ithica: Snowlion Publications, 2006.

Dzigar Kongtrul. *Uncommon Happiness*. Hong Kong: Rangjung Yeshe Publications, 2009.

Erik Pema Kunsang and Marcia Schmidt, trans. *Skillful Grace*. Hong Kong: Rangjung Yeshe Publications, 2007.

Goodman, Steven. *Frogs In The Custard*. Ithica: Snowlion Publications, forthcoming.

Jo Nang Taranatha. *The Origin of Tara Tantra*. Rev. ed. Translated by David Templeton. Dharmsala: Library of Tibetan Works and Archives, 1995.

Kunsang Pelden. *The Nectar of Manjushri's Speech.* Translated by the Padmakara Translation Group. Boston: Shambhala Publications, 2007.

Laird, Thomas. *The Story of Tibet: Conversations with the Dalai Lama.* New
York: Grove Press, 2006

Lerab Lingpa. *The Sphere of Timeless Awareness.* Translated by Richard
Barron. Turquoise Dragon, 1999.

Padmasambhava and Jamgön Kongtrül. *Light of Wisdom.* Translated by
Erik Pema Kunsang. 2 vols. Hong Kong: Rangjung Yeshe Publications,
1993–98.

Padmasambhava *Treasures from the Juniper Ridge.* Erik Pema Kunsang,
trans. Hong Kong: Rangjung Yeshe Publications, 2008.

Patrul Rinpoche. *Words of My Perfect Teacher.* Boston: Shambhala Publications, 1998.

Putsi Pema Tashi. *Teachings on the Trinley Nyingpo 35-Day Retreat,* Translated by Erik Pema Kunsang. Hong Kong: Rangjung Yeshe Translations and Publications, 1998.

Shantideva. *The Way of the Bodhisattva.* Translated by the Padmakara
Translation Group. Boston: Shambhala Publications, 1997.

Thinley Norbu. *A Cascading Waterfall of Nectar.* Boston: Shambhala Publications, 2006.

———. *Magic Dance.* Boston: Shambhala Publications, 1998.

———. *Welcoming Flowers: From Across the Threshold of Hope.* Delhi:
Jewel Publishing, 1996.

Thrangu Rinpoche. *Crystal Clear.* Translated by Erik Pema Kunsang.
Hong Kong: Rangjung Yeshe Publications, 2003.

———. *Songs of Naropa.* Translated by Erik Pema Kunsang. Hong Kong:
Rangjung Yeshe Publications, 1997.

Tsoknyi Rinpoche, *Carefree Dignity,* Translated by Erik Pema Kunsang.
Hong Kong: Rangjung Yeshe Publications, 1998.

Tsultrim Gyatso. *The Practice of Spontaneous Presence.* Translated by Yeshe
Gyamtso. Halifax: Vajravairochana Translation Committee, 1996

Tulku Thondup. *Healing Power of Mind.* Boston: Shambhala Publications,
1998.

———. *Masters of Meditation and Miracles.* Boston: Shambhala Publications, 1995.

Tulku Urgyen Rinpoche. *As It Is.* Translated by Erik Pema Kunsang. 2
vols.

Hong Kong: Rangjung Yeshe Publications, 2000.

———. *Rainbow Painting.* Translated by Erik Pema Kunsang. Hong Kong: Rangjung Yeshe Publications, 1995.

———. *Repeating the Words of the Buddha.* Translated by Erik Pema Kunsang. Hong Kong: Rangjung Yeshe Publications,1992.

———. *Vajra Heart.* Translated by Erik Pema Kunsang. Hong Kong: Rangjung Yeshe Publications, 1988.

Yongey Mingyur Rinpoche. *Joy of Living.* With Eric Swanson. New York: Harmony Books, 2007.

Notes

1   Tulku Urgyen Rinpoche, *Vajra Speech,* 212, defines "a yogi as an individual who connects with that which is naturally so. Yoga means to bring the natural state into actual experience. The one who does this can truly be called a yogi" [or yogini].

2   In the course of the book, I relate certain Dharma awakenings to events in my life. Unfortunately, these experiences do not follow a chronological order, so it may be confusing for the reader to place where I am and what I have been doing. For the sake of clarity, chronologically: I grew up in Philadelphia, where I became a Buddhist, moved to California, where I flirted with radicalism and decided revolution was within, dropped out of University for some years, later completed my degree, moved to a hippie commune and began Zen meditation, became an exercise girl on the race track and broke young race horses on farms, where I learned about mindfulness; and finally moved to Nepal in search of my teacher and have primarily lived there since.

3   Tulku Urgyen Rinpoche, *Vajra Speech,* 122, defines "nature of mind or rigpa as the present moment of unfabricated wakefulness." On page 140 he says, "to recognize it, literally means meeting your nature head-on, to recognize your own essence face-to-face. .... So, what is recognized, is seeing that the nature of mind as an unconfined empty cognizance."

PARADISE LOST

5   The Four Noble Truths are the truth of suffering, the truth of origin, the truth of cessation, and the truth of the path.

6   Tulku Urgyen Rinpoche, (unpublished teaching, October 1991).

7   Tsoknyi Rinpoche, *Carefree Dignity.* 24. This nature of mind is always present, and it can be called different names: the natural state, the basic nature, the real condition, the enlightened essence or buddha nature. This basic nature is what is meant by ground.

8   Thinley Norbu, *A Cascading Waterfall of Nectar,* 20.

9   Ibid., p 23.

10   Chogyam Trungpa, *The Sanity We Are Born With,* 97.

11   Chogyam Trungpa, "Maitri Space Awareness in a Buddhist Thera-
     peutic Community" in *The Collected Works of Chogyam Trungpa,* v. 2,
     562.

12   Steven Goodman, *Frogs, In The Custard,* "And then we have the
     famous five skandhas: 1. Form: the skandha or the grouping called
     'form' consists of ten dharmas, the capacity to see, hear, smell, taste
     and touch, and also what is being perceived or processed, the infor-
     mation, so colors and shapes, sounds, smells, tastes and touch. (We
     might call that channels, *consciousnesses,* 1–5.) Here one does not at
     all pay attention to each single channel. Or rather we just collapse
     channels 1–5 together and say, it's not mind. So of the five skandhas
     only one of them takes care of all those five channels. We are not
     particularly concerned with those five channels. Because the teach-
     ing of the skandhas is said to be for those who think the self is mind;
     mind is one thing. So to them they say, there are things, which are
     not mind. (That is just one skandha.) 2. Sensation: The hallmark in
     doing skandha analysis is to be able to discern the difference between
     form stuff and four precise and different kinds of mind stuff. One
     whole skandha consists of nothing but one energy packet called 'sen-
     sation.' How can one energy packet be an aggregate or a group? It is
     just the energy packet fired by channels 1–6, no matter how it comes.
     But it is all the sensations of pain or pleasure; it is the multiplicity of
     recurring sensation as one whole group. It's all the dharmas of sensa-
     tions from the past, the present and future; that's what the skandha
     is. Not simply of this life. We're stuck with this life. But it will go
     on. 3. Conception: There is also the skandha of being able to sort or
     isolate to have a concept. Every situation of the past, present or future
     has that skandha of conception. It is defined as the capacity to isolate
     or to grab a specific feature. 4. Karmic Formation: Of course most of
     them are in the completely overwhelming skandha known as karmic
     formations. (When I think of formations I think of tin soldiers.) 5.
     Consciousness: Then there is the one which is able to sort out, which
     of course is the one called mind itself. That is the compiler, the guys
     from our dhatu analysis. They make a guest appearance, and that
     is the so-called consciousness skandha. Because mind only operates,
     according to this way of viewing, to compile, to integrate into an
     experience of seeing. In first turning teachings they say that of the

five skandhas it is this last one that transmigrates. It is the vijnana skandha that goes on and on. It is not the form, it is not the sensation, it is not the little bits to pick out. There is some discussion about this." 178.

13 In the glossary to Chogyam Trungpa's *The Sanity We Are Born With,* we find an explanation of this key term: "Rinpoche's use of this term, ego refers to an illusory belief in the solid existence of a self. The belief in a separate self or ego is the fundamental source of suffering and anxiety. It is contrasted with one's basic goodness and buddha nature, which are the genuine ground of self-confidence."

14 Explanations based on unpublished, oral teachings from Tulku Urgyen Rinpoche. Corresponding to the poison of ignorance, the element of space, and in its purified form the Buddha Vairochana.

15 Corresponding to the poison of pride, the element of earth, and the Buddha Ratnasambhava.

16 Corresponding to the poison of attachment, the element of fire, and the Buddha Amitabha.

17 Corresponding to the poison of jealousy, the element of wind, and the Buddha Amoghasiddhi.

18 Corresponding to the poison of anger, the element of water, and the Buddha Akshobya.

19 Tulku Urgyen Rinpoche, *Repeating the Words of the Buddha,* 34

RED OR BLUE PILL

20 Dilgo Khyentse Rinpoche, *Zurchungpa's Testament,* 91.

21 Thrangu Rinpoche, *Song of Naropa* in *Dzogchen Primer,* 236

22 Gyalse Ngulchu Thogme, *The Thirty Seven Verses on the Practices of A Bodhisattva,* verse 24, quoted in, Dilgo Khyentse Rinpoche, *The Heart of Compassion,* 33.

23 Dzongsar Khyentse Rinpoche, "Renunciation Mind," in *Dzogchen Primer,* 45–53.

24 Adeu Rinpoche, (unpublished teachings, Rigpa, San Francisco, USA, October 19, 1999).

25 The Nine Gradual Vehicles are the Hinayana Vehicle that includes Shravaka and Pratyekabuddhas, which focus on contemplation of the Four Noble Truths and the twelve links of dependent origination, the practice of which brings liberation from cyclic existence. The Mahayana Vehicle is the Bodhisattva Vehicle, which includes

the bodhisattva vow to liberate all sentient beings through means and knowledge, compassion, and insight into emptiness. The Vajrayana Vehicle has six divisions: the three outer tantras Kriya, Upa, Yoga, and the three inner tantras Maha Yoga, Anu Yoga, and Ati Yoga. Dzogchen belongs to the Ati Yoga of the Vajrayana Vehicle.

26   Tulku Urgyen Rinpoche, "The View and the Nine Vehicles," *Rainbow Painting*, 33.

THE PATH LESS TRAVELED

27   Tsoknyi Rinpoche, *Carefree Dignity*, 24.
28   Dzigar Kongtrul, *Uncommon Happiness*, 15.
29   Ibid, 63-69.
30   Yongey Mingyur Rinpoche, *Joy of Living*, 47.
31   Ibid., 80.

CONTEMPLATION

32   Gegan means a teacher.
33   As defined by Dilgo Khyentse Rinpoche in *Zurchungpa's Testament*, "Additionally there are the eight intrusive circumstances that cause you to drift away from Dharma: (1) to be greatly disturbed by the five poisonous emotions; (2) to be extremely stupid, and thus easily led astray by unsuitable friends; (3) to fall prey to the devil of a mistaken path; (4) to be distracted by laziness even though you have some interest in Dharma; (5) to lead a wrong way of life, and be afflicted by negative karma; (6) to be enslaved or controlled by others; (7) to practice for mundane reasons, such as just to be protected from danger or out of fear that you might lack food or other basic necessities; and (8) to practice a hypocritical semblance of Dharma in the hope of wealth and fame; and the eight incompatible propensities that limit your natural potential to attain freedom are (1) to be fettered by your family, wealth, and occupations so that you do not have the leisure to practice the Dharma; (2) to have a very corrupt nature that drives you to depraved behavior, so that even when you meet a spiritual teacher it is very hard to turn your mind to Dharma; (3) to have no fear of samsara's sufferings, and therefore no feeling of disillusionment with samsara, or determination to be free from it; (4) to lack the jewel of faith and therefore have no inclination whatsoever to meet a teacher and undertake the teachings; (5) to delight in negative actions and

have no compunction about committing them, thereby turning your back on the Dharma; (6) to have no more interest in Dharma than a dog in eating grass, being therefore unable to develop any positive qualities; (7) to have spoiled your pratimoksha vows and Mahayana precepts, and thus to have nowhere else to go but the lower realms of existence, where there is no leisure to practice the Dharma; and (8) having entered the extraordinary path of the Vajrayana, to break samaya with your teacher and vajra brothers and sisters, and thus be parted from your natural potential" (56).

34 Khandro Rinpoche, (unpublished transcript, 2004).

35 Tulku Urgyen Rinpoche, *Rainbow Painting*, 145–46.

36 For example, Patrul Rinpoche, *Words of My Perfect Teacher.*

THE TEACHER COMPONENT

37 Dzongsar Khyentse Rinpoche, *Dzogchen Essentials*, 96–101.

38 Tulku Thondup, *The Healing Power of Mind*, 166.

39 Patrul Rinpoche, *Words of My Perfect Teacher*, 258.

BODHICHITTA

40 These are not to kill, steal, engage in sexual misconduct; not to lie, use harsh words, speak divisively, engage in idle gossip; and not to have covetousness, ill will, or wrong view.

41 Dilgo Khyentse Rinpoche, *The Heart Treasure of Compassion*, 98–99.

42 Lama Putsi Pema Tashi, *Teachings on the Trinley Nyingpo 35-Day Retreat*, 87.

43 Verse 31 of the Gyalse Ngulchu Thogme's *The Thirty Seven Verses on the Practices of A Bodhisattva* quoted in Dilgo Khyentse Rinpoche, *The Heart of Compassion*, 3.

44 Dzigar Kongtrul Rinpoche, *Uncommon Happiness*, 21, 23, 67, 93.

45 Chokgyur Lingpa, *Ocean of Amrita*, 14.

46 Sylvia Boorstein, "Tamara's Joy," *Shambhala Sun* (May 2008), 25.

47 Dzigar Kongtrul, *Uncommon Happiness*, 65.

48 Tulku Urgyen Rinpoche (unpublished teachings, 1991).

49 Kunzang Pelden, *The Nectar of Manjushri's Speech*, 47.

MEDITATION

50 Chogyam Trungpa, *The Sanity We Are Born With*, 20.

51 Dilgo Khyentse Rinpoche, *Gongyen: The Mind Ornament of*

Samantabhadra, 98.

52   For a very comprehensive explanation of this practice please read *Clarifying the Natural State,* by Dakpo Tashi Namgyal, and *Crystal Clear,* by Thrangu Rinpoche.

53   Tulku Urgyen Rinpoche, *Repeating the Words of the Buddha,* 26.

54   Thrangu Rinpoche, *Songs of Naropa,* 159-161

55   From "The Crystal Garland of Daily Practice," concerning the Mahamudra of the completion stage in the Lama Gongdü cycle, *Treasures from Juniper Ridge,* 68.

HEALING WITH TARA

56   See Erik Pema Kunsang and Marcia Schmidt, trans., *Skillful Grace.* I also received teachings on the *Zabtik Cycle* Tara from Sokse Rinpoche, Tulku Pema Wangyal, and Orgyen Topgyal Rinpoche. I learned the melodies from Mayum Kunsang Dechen, the consort of Tulku Urgyen Rinpoche and the mother of Chokyi Nyima Rinpoche.

57   See, for example, Jo Nang Taranatha, *The Origin of Tara Tantra.* The great Tibetan historian Taranatha (1575 to mid-17th century) is conjectured to have strung together various episodes heard from other sources, probably the main one being his prime Indian teacher Buddhaguptanatha.

58   Orgyen Topgyal Rinpoche, *Skillful Grace,* 20.

59   Tulku Urgyen Rinpoche (unpublished teachings). Answers, Nagi Nunnery, Nepal, 1984.

60   Adeu Rinpoche (unpublished transcript, 2002).

61   Adeu Rinpoche, *Skillful Grace,* 98 and 107.

62   Ibid., 113.

63   Tulku Urgyen Rinpoche (unpublished teachings). Answers, Nagi Nunnery, Nepal, 1985.

64   Tulku Thondup, "The Healing Meditation of Devotion," *Dzogchen Essentials,* 148.

CONDUCT

65   Khandro Rinpoche (unpublished teaching, Mingling Practice and Daily Life, Rangjung Yeshe Gomde, CA., USA, October , 2006).

66   Chogyam Trungpa, *Transcending Madness,* 8.

67   Adeu Rinpoche (unpublished teaching, Rigpa, San Francisco, CA., October 1999).

68 Tulku Urgyen Rinpoche, *Rainbow Painting*, 197.

69 Earlier in the same text, Trungpa Rinpoche defines bardo as "present experience, the immediate experience of nowness—where you are, where you are at" (3).

70 Dilgo Khyentse Rinpoche, *The Heart of Compassion*, 90.

INTEGRATION

71 The five degenerations are "(1) the degeneration of views due to the decline in the virtue of renunciates, meaning wrong views; (2) the degeneration of disturbing emotions due to the decline in the virtue of house-holders, meaning coarse-natured minds in which coarseness refers to strong and long-lasting disturbing emotions; (3) the degeneration of times due to the decline in enjoyments, meaning the decreasing Aeon of Strife; (4) the degeneration of life span due to the decline of the sustaining life-force, meaning a decreasing life span, finally reaching the length of ten years; (5) the degeneration of sentient beings, meaning the decline of body due to inferior shape and lesser size, the decline of merit due to lesser power and splendor, the decline of mind due to lesser sharpness of intellect, power of recollection and diligence. Thus, the degeneration of sentient beings in whom the three types of decline have come together, meaning that their minds are difficult to tame," Jokyab Rinpoche, *The Light of Wisdom, volume 1*, 552.

72 Dzigar Kongtrul, *Uncommon Happiness*, 127.

73 Tulku Urgyen Rinpoche, *As It Is*, v. 2, 236–38.

74 Dzongsar Khyentse Rinpoche, "Calling the Guru from Afar" (oral teaching, Vancouver, B. C. 2004)

75 Tulku Urgyen Rinpoche defines this term in many ways one being, self-existing awareness.

76 For more detailed teachings on these four topics, see *As It Is*, v. 2, 177–80.

77 Adeu Rinpoche, (unpublished teachings, Rigpa, San Francisco, USA, October 19, 1999).

78 Dzongsar Khyentse Rinpoche (oral teaching,). PPI, Jenner, CA. August, 2008, Aspirations. In the *Tegchog Dzo,* Longchenpa suggests different places to practice: (1) In a cemetery, it easier to attain accomplishments. A cemetery keeps you on edge, makes mind fresh. A cemetery is the best for all kinds of meditation. (2) A mountain

peak is good for diligence; a dull person should meditate on the top of a mountain. (3) Near a moving river invokes a sense of urgency in a practitioner, and sadness and renunciation occur easier. (4) Rocky mountain caves raise renunciation mind, as well as both shamatha and vipashyana stability. (5) In the forest there is a better chance for stable mind; shamatha comes easier in the forest, and among the different experiences, blissful experiences will come. (6) Dwelling near a snow mountain is good for development stage and vipashyana meditations, and it also helps with reducing obstacles.

79   His Holiness the Dalai Lama states, "I think that the collective energy of the myriad sentient beings who inhabit the world system shapes the whole universe" (*The Story of Tibet: Conversations with the Dalai Lama* 150).

80   Lerab Lingpa, *The Sphere of Timeless Awareness,* 62–63.

81   Khandro Rinpoche unpublished teaching, Mingling Practice and Daily Life, Rangjung Yeshe Gomde, CA. USA, October 2006.

YES TO POSSIBILITIES

82   Thinley Norbu, *Magic Dance,* 77.

83   Dilgo Khyentse Rinpoche, *The Heart Treasure of Compassion,* 124.

84   Thinley Norbu, *A Cascading Waterfall of Nectar,* 21.

85   Tulku Urgyen Rinpoche (unpublished teaching, 1985).

86   Tulku Urgyen Rinpoche (unpublished teaching, 1985).

87   Khenpo Tsultrim Gyatso, *The Practice of Spontaneous Presence.*

88   Mingyur Rinpoche, *Joy of Living,* 82.

89   Thinley Norbu, *Welcoming Flowers: From Across the Threshold of Hope.* 42.

90   Tulku Urgyen Rinpoche, *Vajra Speech,* 210.

91   Lerab Lingpa, *The Profound Drop of Vimala According to the Great Chetsun,* 170.

92   Op cit

93   Tulku Thondup, *Masters of Meditation and Miracles,* 263.

APPENDIX 1

94   Tulku Urgyen Rinpoche, *Rainbow Painting,* 36.

95   Ibid, 37.

96   Thrangu Rinpoche, *Crystal Clear,* 78 and 81.

97   Tulku Urgyen Rinpoche, *Rainbow Painting,* 35–41

APPENDIX 2

98 A hidden treasure of Chokgyur Dechen Lingpa, translated by Erik Pema Kunsang.

99 Avalokiteshvara.

100 Pani padme.

101 The Sanskrit gives "knit brows

102 Here again various translations differ. We chose the combined meaning of the Sanskrit and the Tibetan.

103 The word *sgrol ma* in Tibetan refers to Tara the Liberator, used in most translations of this line. However, when comparing this with the Sanskrit, my friend Mattia Salvini thinks there was a scribal error and the actual word should have been *sgron ma,* or lamp, hence "illuminate." The Sanskrit is diipite, and it could not have been Tara for metrical reasons.

104 The moon.

105 The literal Sanskrit translation is, "She vanquishes all poisons with the syllable PHAT uttered twice with TARA."

106 Half man and half horse, they can fly and are very good musicians.

Contact Addresses for Teachings and Retreats

FOR INFORMATION REGARDING PROGRAMS and recorded and published teachings in the lineage of Tulku Urgyen Rinpoche, please access one of the following websites:

Shedrub Development Mandala
www.shedrub.org

Rangjung Yeshe Gomdé, USA
www.gomdeusa.org

Rangjung Yeshe Gomdé, Denmark
www.gomde.dk

Rangjung Yeshe Publications
www.rangjung.com